# Open for Liberation

## An activist reads the Bible

What people are saying about

# Open for Liberation

Tim Gee's book is a call to action. Rooted in scripture, he takes us on a compelling journey, reading expressions of liberation, justice and protest through the lens of the poetry, praise and narrative of the Bible. Unafraid to name where scripture has been used to hurt or abuse the vulnerable, Gee paints a vivid picture of a contemplative-activist reading "social change theologically" and asking "How does the Bible read us?" How are we compelled to act for justice? In a world sorely in need of fearless compassionate leadership this compact book spills over with extraordinary inspiration. *Open for Liberation* shines a light on the core practices of what it means to live as a "voice-walker": to "let our lives speak."
**Ruth Harvey**, Leader, The Iona Community

Tim Gee opened himself up to a spiritual walk through scripture – which sounds lovely, doesn't it? That journey, though, challenged long-held assumptions alive and well at the end of centuries of colonial patriarchy. It revealed in Jesus the incarnation of a God of love who opted not for the sentimentality of warm feelings, but for the rebuilding of a world invested in privilege; the dismantling of a world that wields power unjustly based on race, gender, class, or sexual identity; and the redistribution of wealth based on an equity inherent in the godly light with which we are all endowed by our Creator. Read this book with your own open heart and mind and you will see with new eyes the God always before us, known in and as love.
**John C. Dorhauer**, General Minister and President, United Church of Christ

*Open for Liberation* is a stimulating and challenging read. It will be a challenge to those whose view of the Bible is as literal truth, to activists who might regard the Bible as irrelevant, and to those for whom the violence within it is a block to positive reading. Challenging his own reservations and confronting its apparent internal contradictions, Tim Gee's exploration of the Bible reveals his discovery of its beauty, power and truth, and its relevance to all the concerns of our day, from gender and ethnic identity to climate change. *Open for Liberation* provokes the reader to look again, and to find in the Bible a reminder of the spiritual grounding of our action and a radical message for our time.

**Jennifer Kavanagh**, Author of *Practical Mystics* etc.

This book reveals the progressive, inclusive message of the Bible again – a message of good news and liberation for all those who are marginalised, oppressed and seeking justice.

**Ruth Wilde**, National Coordinator, Inclusive Church

# Open for Liberation

An activist reads the Bible

Tim Gee

CHRISTIAN ALTERNATIVE
BOOKS

Winchester, UK
Washington, USA

JOHN HUNT PUBLISHING

First published by Christian Alternative Books, 2022
Christian Alternative Books is an imprint of John Hunt Publishing Ltd.,
No. 3 East St., Alresford, Hampshire SO24 9EE, UK
office@jhpbooks.com
www.johnhuntpublishing.com
www.christian-alternative.com

For distributor details and how to order please visit the 'Ordering' section on our website.

Text copyright: Tim Gee 2020

ISBN: 978 1 78904 236 8
978 1 78904 237 5 (ebook)
Library of Congress Control Number: 2021930335

Design: Stuart Davies

UK: Printed and bound by CPI Group (UK) Ltd, Croydon, CR0 4YY
Printed in North America by CPI GPS partners

We operate a distinctive and ethical publishing philosophy in all areas of our business, from our global network of authors to production and worldwide distribution.

# Contents

Introduction                                    1

1. Lines of Dissent                             8

2. Radical Jesus                               21

3. The Activism of the Apostles               47

Epilogue                                       60

# Introduction

In some progressive movements it has become countercultural to talk about faith. It hasn't always been this way. Many of the great changemakers of history spoke the language of religion and reached their decisions through prayer. Now, though, to make a faith-based case in a meeting about social change can be to break an unspoken rule; that faith and social change should be separated. The mirror of this is in those churches – and there are many – where it is frowned upon to talk about taking public action, which is too often seen as a distraction from the perceived purposes of the community. Even worse, some congregations do engage in social change work, but in a way that serves to perpetuate inequality instead of challenging it. Those that do this, I believe, have either misunderstood or broken with the foundations of our faith.

Christianity in its origins was a movement of the marginalised and the oppressed. It consisted principally of colonised peoples from the Middle East and Africa, suffering under military occupation. Disabled people were central to the movement's growth. The leaders were largely from working-class backgrounds and included both women and men. With time, as it extended to nearby Samaria, it began to resemble an interfaith alliance.

In Jesus we meet a teacher, public speaker and organiser. In modern terms we'd describe him as anti-racist. He's a person who challenges unequal gender norms and affirms sexual diversity. His long walks in nature and words about plants and animals suggest a connection with – and care for – ecology. He also teaches his students to be nonviolent, in defiance of the culture of both his time and ours.

Nowadays people debate whether Jesus is best understood as a religious teacher or as an activist or reformer. It's unlikely this would have made much sense in Jesus' time, as there wouldn't have been such a distinction. Well-known religious texts spoke of the coming of a liberator who would free the country from tyranny. The word that has come to us for this from Hebrew is 'messiah' and from the same word in Greek we have 'Christ'. Today 'liberator', 'messiah' and 'Christ' conjure very different images, but in those times much less so.

Translating concepts between languages is always hard. In the case of the Bible we have the added complication of reaching across different thought-worlds and cultures, separated by millennia. In biblical times, the English language in which I am writing, did not exist, and wouldn't exist for many centuries. Nevertheless, we can still connect, through the spirit that inspires work for justice, which many people involved in social movements today experience too.

One of the people who helped shape my perspective is Scottish activist and former Iona Community peace worker Helen Steven, whose 2005 lecture on activism and prayer remains a source of inspiration. In it she relays her conviction that "we can view Jesus' whole ministry as a life lived in deliberate opposition to the domination of his time. It was not enough to show compassion for the poor and dispossessed, the whole system of oppression which left people in poverty and despair had to be challenged."

I also love reading South African anti-apartheid leader Desmond Tutu, whose ideas are well summarised in his oft-repeated view that "the Bible is the most radical and revolutionary book there is and were a book to be banned by those who rule unjustly then it should have been the Bible." One of his teachers was Black theology pioneer James Cone, who makes central to his understanding the observation that "God did not become a universal human being but an oppressed Jew, thereby disclosing to us that both human nature and divine nature are inseparable from oppression and liberation." Yet these perspectives are not those that are most heard. It often feels as if Christianity has been commandeered for the purposes of winning support for war, racism, sexism and homophobia, all of which goes against the most basic teachings of Jesus. Along with many others, for many years I was put off by all this. Now I believe that a necessary part of the task of liberating humanity from oppression will involve liberating Christianity from those who believe that oppression is consistent with faith.

I first seriously engaged with the Bible when I was 19 during a study visit to Palestine. I took it with me as a kind of travel book, on the basis that it was set around there. On my first night in Jericho I opened up the first of the four accounts of Jesus' life. What I found was something real and relevant: a country under occupation, a movement resisting injustice and debating how best to do so, young people asking how to be good in a system where those in power are engaged in violence, and a critique of war and inequality still applicable today. All this came as a surprise as it seemed very different to what I'd heard people saying it was about.

Another experience, seven years later, transformed my engagement again. I was on a speaking tour with my first book *Counterpower*, during which I attended Quaker Meeting in Philadelphia. They met in silence, only speaking if moved. I found myself meditating on love, the love of family, then of friends then strangers, then I felt a loving force flowing through myself, through everyone in the room, then through everyone in the whole world.

After that, my idea of God shifted from an abstract and confusing concept to a present and tangible feeling. "God is love" became no longer merely a slogan associated with church leaflets on street corners but an experienced truth. So too what the Gospel of John calls the Light, became like a torch which lit up the pages of books about faith. I saw that the scriptures had multiple words for the sense that I felt in that moment, and which I was learning to be able to tune into: the spirit, the word, the truth within, the grace, the wisdom, the seed, the revelation. But at last, I felt comfortable describing this connection as the experience of communion with God. This felt like a whole new language, leading to a reflection on religion. If I hear a group of people conversing in, say, Italian, I don't deny that Italian exists or question its validity just because I don't understand it. I recognise that they are speaking a language I don't, but that with practice I might be able to learn.

Thinking about the analogy of music also helps me. Our ears are trained to recognise whole notes and half notes, and that music is made up from these components. But in fact, there is infinite variety in between – quarter notes, sixteenth notes – all sorts. If I open my mouth to sing them, I am unable, even though I know that in theory they are there. Learning about faith has been about trying to see and hear those things that I screened out previously.

One thing that very quickly became clear, was that in my studies of changemakers through history, I had focussed so much on the strategy and tactics they used, that I had overlooked their perspectives on faith. At the same time, I became aware of how so many Christians seem to ignore or disregard what the Bible has to say about social change.

Today when I open the Bible, I find myself transported into the scene – at times in the crowd at great public meetings, at times in the public gallery doing court support, organising, debating, hoping, despairing. All of the things that form my life as a person committed to making change, I find there in a previous form. I also frequently find myself challenged – we all fall short of the example Jesus set. I'm most challenged by the sections so often pulled out and used out of context, to build support for practices that entrench inequality.

At this point it's worth pausing to reflect on what the Bible is. It's unlikely that many of the authors of its books imagined that one day they would be joined into one. It's better thought of as a library, as in the Latin *bibliotheca*, echoed in the words for library found in Spanish, French, Italian, German, Dutch, Danish, Norwegian and Swedish among other languages. Within this library are many genres of writing: poetry, history, mythology, memoir, fable, biography, novellas, song lyrics, philosophy, letters and legal documents such as land claims. Parts of it even read very much like a construction manual (if you're wondering what I'm talking about, try reading Exodus 37–39).

If we expect every word to be literally true, then we will be sorely disappointed. None of the books in this library are either science or natural history. That didn't stop one Bishop from counting up all the dates in it and proclaiming the world's start date as 4004 BCE. Now, though, scientists think that the world is around four billion years old.

We also need to hold in mind that these are texts that have been translated and retranslated over centuries, changing their interpretations as they go, so much so that even versions of the same words can seem to have different meanings according to which translation you use. Add to this the consideration that there's a strong likelihood that parts have been added and removed through time. Furthermore, the books' authors disagree with one another, in specifics and fundamentals, so much so that it's hard to agree with them all at once. Put together there's a strong biblical case against what gets called biblical literalism.

On the other hand, if we treat the Bible like a visit to a library or a museum of ancient texts, then we free ourselves to engage with different insights, perspectives, understandings and experiences. In such a context we would expect inconsistencies between different versions of the same events – and might be surprised at how similar the different versions are. We don't need to agree with every word we read, every song lyric we hear or every exhibit we see, but by listening and reading widely we can find our way through to a deeper truth within.

And through all this there is a common theme. Popular writer Karen Armstrong tells the story of first-century Rabbi and scholar

Hillel (who as it happens was grandfather to Saul/Paul's teacher Gamaliel) who was challenged to recite the entire Torah while standing on one leg. He stood on one leg and replied "what is hateful to yourself do not do to your fellow man. That is the whole of the Torah and the remainder is but commentary. Go study it". Similarly, Jesus taught that the commandments to love God and love your neighbour as yourself summarised all scripture. So strong is this theme that the fifth-century theologian Augustine of Hippo taught that if any part of the Bible seems to go against this rule, "we must meditate on what we read until an interpretation be found that tends to establish the reign of charity".

Writer and mystic Richard Rohr recommends a process for this: Begin by offering a prayer for guidance (I find Psalm 1 helpful) or alternatively take a moment of stillness and try to listen for a deeper voice than your own. Next read, and listen for what that voice is saying. If what comes leads to love, joy, peace, patience, kindness, goodness, trustfulness, gentleness and self-control then trust it as coming from the spirit. However, if it leads to any sense of superiority, self-satisfaction, desire for revenge, need for victory or tendency towards exclusion, then this is the ego at work.

Most of all we need to avoid interpretations that entrench inequality. In the words of contextual theologian Anthony Reddie: "racism, sexism, patriarchy, homophobia, ageism, classism, among other things all intrinsically deny the love of God because their perpetrators fail to love the wisdom of God that has given them opportunities to love their neighbour." What I take from this is that if our faith ever seems to be justifying violence or discrimination then we haven't thought about it enough.

Thankfully there is a way for us to engage in this thought that doesn't require us to have all of the answers. Liberation theologians often speak of *praxis* – that is a process that all can engage in of action and reflection, action and reflection, repeated infinite times. It was through this kind of thought that this book began. I'd recently moved to working part-time, and was spending my non-work days walking with a pocket Bible tucked into my bag. I walked a bit, read a bit, walked a bit, read a bit, then wrote things down when I got home. Then came the 2020 lockdown during which I started typing things up, leading to the text that follows.

Like all writing, this book is a work in progress. When we speak of believing in science what we mean is that we trust in a process of constant experimentation, leading to insights on an underlying truth, which will always be limited and improvable. As Thomas Merton advised of his writings, the purpose of a book of meditations is not to tell you what to think, as it may be that God wants you to end up somewhere else.

And here I should offer some kind of disclaimer. I don't have all the answers. The process of reading the Bible in its totality has emphasised to me how much I have to learn. On occasion I've noticed that very smooth, agreeable, eloquent presentations about the Bible can have the effect of leading me to doubt, as I ask myself "if someone else already has all the answers, then why would I search myself?" My hope then is that what follows will be sufficiently clumsy, objectionable and inelegant to prompt questions, as it is precisely in the gaps, incompleteness, apparent contradictions and challenges to our beliefs that we find openings to divine insight.

I believe that we each have a measure of the Light. That means anyone who connects with and thinks about God is "doing theology", anyone who shares the fruits of their discernment is giving ministry and anyone who then takes action on it is acting in a prophetic way. My aim is to recognise and foster this by sharing what has arisen in me, as a prompt to see what emerges through you.

## Chapter 1

# Lines of dissent

### In the beginning

"In the beginning was the word, and the word was with God, and the word was God." These are the famous opening lines of the Gospel of John, building on the older opening of Genesis: "In the beginning God created the heavens and the Earth ... and God said 'let there be light' ... and God saw that it was good."

These words have become so caught up in culture wars that it can be hard to appreciate their radical significance. If you struggle with the idea of a God we cannot see, then the words become even harder. God though, we are told, is love. Read this way then, "the word" was love. Love created the heavens and the Earth. Everything is made out of love, by the cosmic embodiment of love.

Why is it that these words move me? They move me because they shift my perspective. Often, I find myself in the details and minutiae of everyday life, but these words invite us to zoom right out and gaze down on the earth from a position outside of space or time, to which we can connect through the love in us all.

To me this experience invites a question: how might the cosmic embodiment of love view us and the ways we organise our societies? What might love have to say about the fact that we humans have enough food for everyone many times over, yet some people starve while others have too much? What might love have to say about environmental damage, species extinction and climate breakdown?

But in the beginning, long before the degradation of present times, the story tells us, "God saw that it was good". These stories are not science. They are prologues delivered in poetry

– or perhaps heightened prose – reflections of wisdom passed down across generations. I'm in awe of how these millennia-old stories so closely prefigure the science of our time.

In the biblical version, God creates the light, the waters, the plants, the animals and once that's all done creates humans. Today we say our ecosystem evolved through infinite interactions. But consider, what is love but an interaction which is infinite? The world we know developed through cosmic community. The first human in the story, Adam (which means "earth") is created out of dust. This human is then divided into two for fear they would be lonely otherwise. Eve (which means "life") is created. In this I read a warning against individualism. We are most whole when in community.

Today we also speak of the universe coming from a "big bang" which means scientists begin speaking like poets: we are every one of us made up of stardust. How beautifully the Bible says something similar. First Genesis: "God said let there be Light". Then John: "This was the true Light that enlightens every person" and elsewhere "God is Light". We are every one of us made of Light and have something of God within us.

Again, the implications are profound. If this is so, then no person should harm another, because doing so would be to harm the divine. So too, humans share more with the non-human world than some would like to admit.

The story of how Adam and Eve live does sound very good. They live in harmony with nature in the Garden of Eden, eating fruit from the trees and roots from the ground, and drinking from the clean unpolluted river. As many reformers have pointed out since, there were no inequalities – not of gender, not of race, not of class.

But like many good stories, within it comes a warning. To maintain the balance with their surroundings, they are told that some of the garden must be left wild. But the humans get greedy and give in to temptation; they start to harvest what should have been left to grow free. Their relationship with the planet is put out of kilter, and they are cast out of the garden, and their lives and those of their children become harder as a result. These are the stories that underpin Christian care for creation. I remember when Britain's gathered Quaker community agreed together to make environmental action central to what we do, we were encouraged by a lecture by educator Pam Lunn. She spoke movingly of the profound and powerful impact of the early colour photographs from space of our lonely home planet, including the famous "Earthrise" image which changed how people thought and helped catalyse the environmental movement. She also recalled how the crew of the same spacecraft as had sent that photo, were asked to give the 1968 Christmas Eve broadcast. As they circled the earth, they contemplated what they should say. In the end they landed on some immortal lines: "In the beginning God created the heavens and the Earth … and God saw that it was good."

## The flood

When I was finding my way into books about faith, I found Symon Hill's *No-Nonsense Guide to Religion* a reassuring companion. Taking in the breadth of religious texts he suggests that even if parts of them are more myth than history "anyone who has read a powerful novel or been deeply affected by a film can testify that a fictional account can convey a truthful point. The meaning of a myth goes beyond its content and is primarily about the context in which it is used."

One of the best-known stories of the Bible begins with the news that the earth has become corrupt and full of violence. Because of this God decides to reset things, and causes a flood across the earth. Beforehand he tells a man called Noah to build a boat for his family and at least two of every creature on the planet, in which they sail for many days and nights, until the flood dies down at which point God promises to never do such a thing again.

Calling this history feels risky. We're told that Noah was nearly 600 years old at the time which suggests more the cadences of the exuberant storyteller than the facts of the sober historian. We might enquire just how so many animals fit on a boat of the proportions laid out, or indeed what became of the plants and how they survived if they were not brought aboard too. It does seem like there may have been a major flood in the area from which the story came, but not one that spanned the entire world as the story recounts. But listing logical shortcomings in non-literal stories is no way to enjoy them or learn. Over years it's been used as a teaching story, an allegory with a moral at its heart. Even then, though, the text raises questions. We could glean that God likes animals and doesn't like violence. But what about all the animals and humans who weren't rescued? Why punish so many for what humans had done? It was while all this was in my mind that I read a string of classic sci-fi novels: First *War of the Worlds,* then *Day of the Triffids,* later Octavia Butler's *Parable of the Talents.* Each of these tells of apocalyptic events in the past tense, as if they have already happened. Some of their depictions have proven unnervingly prescient in general if not in specifics. Of course, this is fiction, not prediction. Nevertheless, there is a truth within each of these novels that patterns of injustice exist in our times and major problems could result.

And then I read Noah's Ark again. Yes. This too reads like a prophetic warning, told through the medium of story. Then I replayed Symon Hill's words back to myself: "The meaning of a myth goes beyond its content and is primarily about the context in which it is used." My context is a world that is unnaturally heating, in which forecasts of a world that is four, five or six degrees hotter, would lead to life on earth being unthinkably different, partly due to severe flooding. Could Noah's story be a prompt to change our ways, and live with more regard for other people and nature?

Noah's story ends happily, the family survives and repopulates the earth. God demands humans not kill one another, nor consume the blood of any animal, in return for which God promises that he will never again destroy all life. We have to hope that we learn from this story, so that ours ends as happily too.

## Abram and Sarai

I have very mixed feelings about the British Museum, but while it is there, I sometimes go. One of the artefacts that fascinates me is from the Mesopotamian city of Ur. One side shows a class system: at the bottom, land workers carrying loads and bringing forth offerings, at the top the elite, drinking with the king. On the other side is the same king commanding an army, as if underlining the nexus between inequality and war. The image sticks in my mind because it feels so current. It also interests me because that same city is mentioned in the Bible as the homeland of Noah's descendants, including Abram and his wife Sarai. Their story begins with the inward call to move away from Ur, first to the smaller city of Haran, and then beyond, to found a new nation of justice.

Until I found that object in the museum, I was content with the story as it stood. This picture of Ur, though, made me ask if there was more. Was it just that they wanted to make a better life elsewhere, or was there something they were escaping from as well? An acute class system propped up by a military seems a long way away from the ideal of the Garden of Eden. Were they moving to avoid being forced to join the military? Or did they want to get out of a system in which the lives of the poor were spent serving the rich? Today I imagine tabloids would label them either "conchies" or "economic migrants" from Iraq. Unfortunately for Abram and Sarai, very little seems to go right. Following a famine, they have to seek sanctuary in Egypt, where Sarai is made a concubine to the country's ruler. When he discovers they are married they are both deported. They then fall out with their nephew who is travelling with them, and they go their separate ways. And through all this they repeatedly fail to conceive, in spite of their dream of a land populated by their descendants.

I read them as hopeful idealists, setting out to build a fairer society from scratch rather than trying to reform an unreformable system. Against the odds they manage to conceive in old age after changing their names to Abraham and Sarah. But they never see the results of their actions, nor do their children or grandchildren. Famine still periodically sweeps the land and their great-grandchildren have to seek sanctuary in Egypt again. Like many utopian projects, the road was lined with setbacks. But they saw not in human time, but in God-time, holding faith that in generations to come they would be parents to a new way of doing things. And they were: first Judaism, then Christianity, followed by Islam, together comprise the Abrahamic faiths. Today nearly half the world's population walks with them.

## Freedom from slavery

My favourite genre of book is autobiography, usually of people working for change. My first was Nelson Mandela's *Long Walk to Freedom* which had me rapt from beginning to end. The one I've read most is Martin Luther King Jr's story, compiled from his speeches and papers. I value them so much because, as I try to make change in the ways that I can, I feel reassured and inspired by their struggles and successes.

I feel much the same – but more so – with the books of Moses in the Bible which tell of the long walk to freedom of the Hebrew people from slavery in Egypt to their long dreamed-of Promised Land. They are led by Moses, a leader who faces recognisably human challenges: he struggles with doubt and comes into conflict with people who want to continue the old ways of doing things.

At times he lacks self-confidence, especially in public speaking. The story begins in Egypt where the Hebrews are suffering greatly. They are forced to work without pay, are beaten, whipped, accused of disloyalty and abused with what we'd now call racial slurs. At intervals, new children are taken away from their parents and killed.

One of those children would have been Moses. He escapes this fate when he is adopted by the daughter of Pharaoh. He lives a privileged life, effectively the grandson of the ruler of the country, benefiting from oppression. Whilst walking in the wilderness, though, he realises that he owes it to his people to help liberate them. This revelation comes to him through a presence he can't quite comprehend, which describes itself only as "I am who I am".

Moses returns to the capital to demand that his people be released. When Pharaoh refuses, ten catastrophes plague the country, each one interspersed with freedom demands. Eventually the people walk out. They cross the Red Sea – read by some as the "Sea of Reeds". When Pharaoh's army follows with their heavy chariots they sink in the mud and get no further. Here is one of the world's superpowers with an overweening military, immobilised by their own hubris. The part of the Bible thought to be the oldest is a freedom song about the event.

Free at last, Moses' people still have to walk for forty years. Alongside his brother Aaron, Moses lays down the law in the wilderness to keep the community healthy and united. The first generation dies out, including Moses who is taken to the top of a mountain to see the Promised Land, but never makes it in person. But the people carry on led by Joshua to reach their destination, beginning with Jericho whose walls collapse after being encircled by the group.

There's good reason to question whether events occurred exactly as depicted, but that's no reason to dismiss the story outright. Thousands of years later the narrative still creates history, because it still inspires struggles for change. Organised workers still say to their bosses, that if they aren't treated well, they'll walk out, often preceded by smaller but escalating actions. Movements still try to support a transition from environmental catastrophe towards a world that is based on justice.

And so it has been through different freedom struggles, where the link has often been explicit. Anti-slavery leader Harriet Tubman was known by the nickname "Moses". Anti-apartheid leader Albert Luthuli called his memoir *Let My People Go*. Leaders of the struggle for civil rights in the USA used the story of Jericho to emphasise the efficacy of nonviolent marches and Mahalia Jackson sang *Joshua Fit the Battle of Jericho* at freedom rallies. Martin Luther King Jr's companion Ralph Abernathy called his autobiography *And the Walls Came Tumbling Down*.

And then there is King whose final speech, on the eve of his assassination spoke of "God's children in their magnificent trek from the dark dungeons of Egypt through, or rather across the Red Sea, through the wilderness on toward the Promised Land." God's children represented the movement. The wilderness represented their setbacks. But he finished his public ministry on a note of hope: "I've been to the mountaintop ... I've seen the Promised Land. I may not get there with you. But I want you to know tonight, that we, as a people, will get to the Promised Land!"

## Power

Something I love about the Hebrew scriptures is that the lessons aren't always spelled out. The Jewish tradition of *midrash* encourages the reader to go beyond surface meanings into the transformative possibilities that can be found within. I like the respect that this affords to the reader, as we are treated as capable of nuance. The characters in the texts are not necessarily faultless role models, but complicated humans who do good and bad.

It's worth holding this in mind as we continue through the books of Joshua, Judges, Samuel, Kings and Chronicles. In these books we read of the conquest of the Promised Land, its rule by judges, then the monarchies of Saul, David and Solomon after which the country starts to splinter. Along with the books of Ecclesiastes and Proverbs, the Song of Songs and the Psalms, these books show these rulers' best and worst qualities, on one hand capable of great wisdom, poetry, song-writing and statecraft, on the other hand susceptible to temptation, adultery, jealousy and violence.

These aren't easy documents to read, not because of their style, but their content. Alongside the stories of ancient Israel's leaders, we're also told of massacres of entire ethnic groups following the battle of Jericho, extreme violence against women and girls, gory details of the chopping up of victims' bodies and even an instance where a hundred enemies' foreskins are demanded as a dowry. How do we read these disturbing words in a way that leads to the reign of charity?

Again, historians have cast doubt on this being exactly how things happened – the archaeological record suggests the land was originally peacefully settled – but that's little comfort when we know that some so-called Christians originating in Europe have used the texts to justify persecution of indigenous peoples in the Americas, Oceania, Africa and Asia, casting themselves as the Israelites wiping out the "heathen" in the lands they were invading. The fact the books tell stories of battles between Israelites and Philistines in places where Israelis and Palestinians are in conflict today, makes it all the more uncomfortable.

At this point I had to stop reading. It was too much, too real. It was then that I re-visited the context of how these books were compiled. The Bible as we know it began taking shape around the sixth century BCE. Before that the centre of the Hebrew world was the temple in Jerusalem. But Jerusalem had been invaded, the temple destroyed, and its people were living in exile in Babylon. Some scrolls had been salvaged, the stories and songs of oral tradition were remembered and new histories began to be written.

The purpose of these efforts was twofold. Partly it was to sustain the culture of a colonised people, and to ensure the original teachings of justice and fairness were not forgotten. It was also to ask how this could have happened. How could the followers of the only monotheistic faith in the world, who believed their homeland was promised by God, find themselves so separated from it?

That was when I realised that I'd been reading it all wrong. The most disturbing parts of these accounts needn't be read as actions to be emulated. Instead, a little like a human rights report – or perhaps an official enquiry – we can read them as histories to be recorded and remembered, in order to avoid the repetition of their most violent elements. Where the exact events were unknown, for example, some of the border wars which took place, stories representing them were used.

Faith communities, social movements and nations like to remember the best things about their pasts, and sometimes play down or even forget the times they haven't got it right. I'm conscious, for example, that the Quaker community I am part of takes pride in having campaigned against slavery, segregation and colonialism but less often talks about those earlier Quakers who fell short in their understandings of racial justice. I imagine every faith group will have their equivalents.

But forgetting about injustice doesn't make it go away. It is only when we identify patterns of harm that we are able to take action to address them. Rather than brushing the past under the carpet, in the Bible we find a different way of doing things. We need to remember both the good and the bad from our histories, so we can learn and make change for the future.

## Prophets

Following many a demonstration, comes the time for rally speeches. Invariably some of these will speak to our condition more than others. Even if we don't attend in person, we'll be familiar with some from history. A few years ago, a friend suggested I try reading the words of the biblical prophets as protest oratory. This approach was transforming. Imagining listening to each one proclaiming their words from a platform, gave these millennia-old words a sense of urgent energy, passion and contemporary relevance.

One of the earliest of the prophets is Amos who begins by emphasising he is not an ordained priest, but a shepherd. In the book that bears his name he declares that the powerful have forgotten the foundations of their faith in social justice, and are instead prioritising ritual over compassion. In words famously echoed in Martin Luther King Jr's 1963 *I Have a Dream* speech, Amos calls for justice to roll down like waters and righteousness like a mighty stream.

Hosea builds on the theme. In his book he condemns the war crimes of the surrounding nations but says his own country is at fault as well. He calls out murder and corruption, the merchant who "uses dishonest scales and loves to defraud" and those who boast "I am very rich; I have become wealthy". He also mourns the dying of mammals, birds and fish and dreams of a day when the instruments of killing both people and animals will be abolished for ever.

Isaiah's message is similar. He too says he's had enough of animal sacrifices and also speaks of a time when people "will beat their swords into ploughshares and their spears into pruning hooks." Similar words appear in the testimony of Micah who demands people "do justly, love mercy, and walk humbly with God".

Habakkuk speaks of the treachery of wealth, warns rich people who live in big houses that "the very stones in the walls cry out" against them and speaks of a coming debt rebellion. He also declares that the time will soon come to expose those who cut down the forests and destroy the wild animals.

Ezekiel records a vision of the spirit of God travelling from their former land to join the community in exile. After a change in imperial politics, Ezra and Nehemiah recount the rebuilding of the faith community in Jerusalem, calling out those rich people re-enslaving the labourers. They make everyone sign a covenant agreeing to pay their taxes and to cancel all debts every seven years.

There is a powerful strand of gender equality through the books. Isaiah points to the hypocrisy of shaming women for sleeping with more than one man when men do the same the other way. Elsewhere he speaks of God as a nursing mother. Jeremiah goes further, speaking of a day when relations between men and women will be transformed. This builds on the books of Ruth and Esther, which tell stories of principled women doing good, even while the male, rich and powerful are engaged in injustice.

In Zephaniah we find a message of international solidarity and racial justice, as the writer speaks of people of God in sub-Saharan Africa with whom the exiles must unite. Joel makes clear that all people will have access to the Holy Spirit. Malachi has a specific warning for priests whose words lead people to harm others: I will "splatter your faces with the manure from your festival sacrifices"!

The Hebrew scriptures which many Christians call the Old Testament, have been used to justify oppression. Taken as a whole, though, the message is the opposite. The very word Hebrew, "the people from over the river", refers to the marginalised. Again and again, God sides with the oppressed. As Psalm 146 has it (echoed by Isaiah) in the King James Version: "The Lord preserveth the strangers, he relieveth the fatherless and the widow, but the way of the wicked he turneth upside down." Abraham, Moses and the prophets, all sought to turn wicked ways upside down. In turn they set the mould for another radical, the one known to us as Jesus.

# Chapter 2

# Radical Jesus

## Origins

If things had been different, perhaps Joseph would have been King. He was the many-times-grandson of David and Solomon and could trace his ancestry back to Abraham. But he wasn't King. He was a low-income labourer. Judea and Samaria were under military occupation and were now a backwater of the Roman Empire. The empire was ruled by Augustus, the adoptive son of Julius Caesar who was considered by some as divine. According to imperial religion, the Emperor was "Son of God".

Locally, Rome appointed a man named Herod to be "King of the Jews", who passed on his rule to his sons after his death. Herod spearheaded a significant construction programme, including rebuilding the Jerusalem Temple. But whatever respect he gained from this act, he lost by erecting a Roman eagle outside it. Taxes from locals paid for this work, with the leftover sent for the use of the Romans to fund the very soldiers who oppressed them. Many people fell into debt.

Unsurprisingly there was resistance, especially in Galilee which was known as a hotbed of revolt. Part of the authoritarian infrastructure of the time was the census. In 6 CE there was a rebellion against it led by Judas the Galilean (not to be confused with Judas Iscariot). He was said to be the son of the freedom fighter Hezekiah who had led a guerrilla war some 40 years before, and father in turn to Menahem ben Judah who would later fight to liberate the land from Roman rule.

Herod also faced an uprising led by one of his former slaves, named Simon, who succeeded in looting and burning down the royal palace in Jericho. Soon afterwards, a young shepherd named Athronges continued the insurrection, including by ambushing columns of Roman soldiers. It's likely these revolts sought to emulate events of more than a century before when rebel warriors reclaimed Jerusalem from the Seleucid Empire which had enforced Greek culture on their homeland. All of this serves as context for a reading of the gospels which takes the political turmoil of the period into account. It begins with what we know as the Christmas story: Joseph is in love with a young woman called Mary who becomes pregnant. They travel from Galilee to Bethlehem to register for the census. On arrival, place after place tells them there's no room at the inn. They sleep in a barn where Mary gives birth and lays her child in a cattle trough. But then the word gets out.

The first people to visit arrive under cover of nightfall. Like Abraham, Amos and Athronges they work as shepherds. They have read that a descendant of David will liberate the land again, and knowing Joseph's ancestry, they celebrate the birth. A few days later a trio of very rich men arrives, bringing with them expensive gifts. If I think myself into the scene, I can see why this might have raised the parents' suspicions. Why would these very wealthy people visit them? And with gold and hugely expensive oils?

If that was their hunch, they were right. When Herod had heard about the birth, he had enrolled the three rich men as spies. But after meeting the family their consciences get the better of them, and they return to their homeland by another route. Joseph and Mary escape the country too, and become refugees in Egypt.

The text offers some clues as to Mary's political outlook. When Mary becomes pregnant, she sings a song describing God as one who brings down rulers from their thrones, lifts up the humble, fills the hungry with good things and sends the rich away empty. In this context the parents' choices of names for their children are particularly interesting. We know the names of four of Jesus' brothers: James, Joseph, Judas and Simon. Could it have been that the youngest two were named after Judas the Galilean and Simon the slave rebel?

This leads us naturally to ask about the name of Mary's first child. The prophecy had been that he would be called Immanuel. Instead, they call him Yeshua as in Joshua – the man who led the Hebrews into Jericho, translated into Greek as Jesus. Why would the one the prophets said would be called "Prince of Peace" be named after a military man? It might have been unconscious, but it seems it fulfilled the other part of the prophesy: In his name swords are turned into ploughshares.

## John the Baptist

Anyone who has been involved in social movements will be familiar with divides between different factions. This is not new. In first-century Palestine historians note myriad sects, each of which approached power differently. Some of the most militant were known as zealots. There were also Pharisees – led by lower- and middle-class religious teachers who interpreted the scriptures for the masses. More conservative were the Sadducees whose leaders were often wealthy landowners and much more accommodating to empire. Most compromised of all were the Scribes (legal scholars) who profited most from injustice.

In addition, there was also a group who did things differently, known as the Essenes. They lived peaceably but separately from Roman society. Some lived alone and others in communes where they shared their property in common. They had a ritual of fully immersing themselves in water, in order to maintain purity, as well as a water-based ritual of initiation. They rejected the religious hierarchy, didn't sacrifice animals, and lived their lives as well as they could in anticipation of a great change to come.

This is useful context to hold in mind when we read about John the Baptist, a slightly older relative of Jesus. He lives in the wilderness, forages his own food and refuses to eat red meat (sometimes I read him as "John the purist" or "the purifier"). Even though he lives apart from society, people travel to hear him. If people are convinced of what he has to say, he symbolically washes them in the river. He says that a leader will soon emerge who will be far greater than he is.

When Pharisees and Sadducees come to see him, he calls them untrustworthy snakes, and demands that they change their ways. When ordinary people come to his talks he speaks very differently, even if their jobs relate to the occupation. When some tax collectors ask how they could be liberated, he advises them not to collect any more than they absolutely have to. When everyday soldiers come to consult him, he advises them to not take bribes and to do violence to no one.

Another of his listeners is Jesus, who had returned from Egypt after the death of Herod. Jesus pleads that he too be initiated to the movement. John hesitates, perhaps afraid for the danger it would put Jesus in. He bargains that instead Jesus could do the ritual for him, as if looking for some kind of compromise. But Jesus insists and in the end John agrees.

As Jesus turns 30 – the same age as the traditions of the time allowed priestly ministry to begin – he is formally initiated into the movement. From this point on there is no going back. Already at risk from government violence, now he has chosen to join forces with one of the most prominent radicals in the country. As he is lowered into the river, a dove passes over their heads and a great thunderstorm begins.

I think many people with a critique of our unjust society would feel an affinity with John. There were plenty of people who ridiculed him for his choices, but even in the wilderness he begins building the future, modelling the new society in the shell of the old. And the story poses a question for all changemakers: when is the time to withdraw and live prophetic yet peripheral lives? And when is the time to live as part of the messiness of communities, ready to turn the tables if necessary?

## Wilderness

Almost as soon as most of us are born, society's ideas are imposed upon us. Somebody says "it's a boy", "it's a girl", or occasionally "they're intersex". We're assigned a nationality and assumed to have a race which will shape how we're treated through our lives. These combine to form a mask, which grows into a lens, which shapes how we each see the world.

As we grow, however, we each face the question "Who am I?" Are we only the characteristics ascribed to us by others, or is there something beneath it all which wants to emerge, through and as our full selves? Sometimes it is only when we are removed from familiarity that these questions begin to be answered.

We may well see something similar – albeit infinitely more intense – when we read of Jesus' inward struggle. Could he really be who people said he was? The question comes to a head when John is arrested and imprisoned before being killed in custody. All of his life Jesus had been told his destiny. He asks for time alone and goes walking in the mountains. For five weeks he wrestles with the most giant of questions.

He finds a resting place where he sits for a very long time. He finds himself asking, if he is who people say he is, why can't he turn stones into bread? He sits with this question until an answer comes: that people don't live from bread alone, but from the presence of God. He walks on to an even higher place and feels a temptation to jump, thinking that if he is who people say he is then angels will catch him.

But before he can jump, he stops himself, and remembers what his forebears had taught: Do not put God to the test. Then he climbs to an even higher place and looks out across the land. I imagine him looking down on Herod's palace in Jericho and wondering whether if he works within the system

– maybe if he studies to be a Scribe or collaborates with the Roman Empire – then perhaps he could gain personal power and riches. Perhaps eventually he could even become Rome's client ruler himself. At this thought he becomes appalled with himself for considering it and resolves instead to do what his people ask of him. Then he feels a great peace within himself, which is matched with a great determination, and he begins the long descent from the mountaintop to start his work of organising in the towns.

The theme of wilderness runs right through the Bible. Abram and Sarai leave the city for the wilderness. Moses encounters God in the wilderness. Isaiah prophesies of "a voice crying in the wilderness". John and Jesus fulfil this tradition, which continued long afterwards too. Christianity's "desert fathers" were rebels against religious hierarchy who sought their own relationship with the divine. The Greek word for wilderness comes from the word hermit.

One expression of this impulse is walking or journeying, and its spiritual extension: pilgrimage. But the 2020 lockdown has made me think differently. Those of us who have needed to self-isolate or shield have found ourselves in the wilderness from our daily routines, even whilst staying indoors. It's a time that has felt difficult, even desolate at times. But wherever we are we can go on journeys of the heart. We all need the wilderness sometimes.

## The beginnings of the movement

Not long after my spiritual experience in Philadelphia, I began working for a faith-based NGO as a campaigner for climate justice. There I worked every day with people whose faith was manifested in action to make the world fairer. At intervals they would produce documents exploring this, led by theologian and United Reformed Church minister Susan Durber.

Central to her approach, which she encouraged in us, was the recognition that theological thinking starts in different places for different people, explaining that privilege, when we have it, will always distort our thinking and require the seeking, with humility, of the wisdom of others. This approach influenced me profoundly.

I held it in mind when reading about US Civil Rights activist Barrington Dunbar, who was disturbed by the complacency about racism he observed in white majority churches. Returning from an ecumenical conference he wrote a paper explaining how he understood his faith. He described Jesus as one with a "revolutionary strategy, who gathered together a disciplined people in his effort to share with them his vision of the beloved community, of the Kingdom of God, freed from the barriers of race, clan or creed".

I hold this in mind when I read the story of Jesus building his team, beginning with two fishermen who he knows through John the Baptist's movement. Together they recruit others and spread what they call the "good news" (in Greek: *gospel*) – a daring choice of words given the term was usually used for imperial announcements about new Emperors and kings. But the Kingdom they speak of would have no human ruler, but would exist for the poor, provide health services for the sick and free people from prison.

The word spreads, and soon there are great crowds coming to listen. We get a clue about who is in this new movement from the way Jesus starts his most famous speech which he begins by greeting and blessing a series of people. Allowing for cross-cultural translation we could read these groups as being the working class ("the poor"), people who are sad about how things are ("those who mourn"), people committed to nonviolence ("the meek"), activists ("those who hunger and thirst for righteousness"), pacifists ("the peacemakers"), more privileged people who try to act kindly ("the merciful") and people committed to living lives uncontaminated by empire ("the pure in heart"). In other words, it looks not dissimilar to a progressive public meeting today.

Translating directly from Aramaic into English, Palestinian priest Elias Chacour points out that in Jesus' native language the word rendered into English as "blessed" is not some passive term. Instead, it means something like "get up, go ahead, do something, move". Were Jesus a social movement leader today I hear him beginning his speech by declaring "Rise up and take action fellow people of the working class."

This puts the rest of the speech in context. Jesus calls his hearers the "salt of the earth": the people with the power, the talent and the determination to make a change, and who could show to the world just what it could do. But this movement would be about more than mere politics. Instead, it would call for a change in culture, attitudes, and the actions of participants. It would mean being reliable, keeping promises, and forgiving one another when people fall short. It would mean not shouting at comrades, and trying to settle conflicts in the movement through conciliation rather than more litigious processes. It would mean not retaliating if a fight looks likely to start, but instead breaking the cycle of violence and escalation, by choosing not to hit back.

And it would mean full respect for women – no gawping or wolf-whistling (a rhetorical flourish here when he said he would rather men tossed their eyes away or chopped off their hands than engage in such actions). Men must also end the practice of cheating on their partners or leaving their wives for younger women, especially if it left their former wives destitute.

To those listeners who either are or who want to be rich, he warns "you cannot serve both God and money". To those planning on doing good just to look good in front of others (today it might be called "performative activism" or "optical allyship") he warns that no real good would come of it. And to those who do these things but get all morally superior and "judgy" about it, he warns that this would be a sure-fire way to get people to judge them in return.

All-in-all he describes a movement that practises what it preaches ("First get rid of the log in your own eye; then you will see well enough to deal with the speck in your friend's eye."). And while he does condemn the rich, the greedy, the scoffers and hypocritical "respectable sorts", he also asks his followers to love them, pray for them, forgive them and refuse to pay evil for evil.

For those of us active in contemporary movements, the advice remains relevant. So too is the recognition that those who oppose us will send spies and agent provocateurs, and others will try to co-opt us. But soon enough we'll know who's who, on account of what they do.

Sometimes I imagine his listeners roaring with applause. Sometimes I sense them in a quiet, respectful stillness as the significance of his words sinks in. Either way, one thing is for sure, he sounded nothing like the religious leaders and politicians they were used to.

## A social view of disability

A few years ago I was running an activist gathering, after which I accompanied a participant in a wheelchair to the nearest train station. On the way the pastor of the church that had been meeting next door rushed out and promised her she would be able to walk if she joined his congregation. She burst into tears, knowing it was untrue and at the pain of having been taken in by such untruths before. The pastor was presumably doing what he thought was right, but seemed to have read the miracle stories of the New Testament in a way which did not lead to justice.

Conscious of this, as part of preparing this book, I searched for readings of the miracle stories by disabled people. Several people had mentioned the problematic interpretations in which Jesus appears to be going round "fixing" people, including by "casting out their sins". Knowing my interest, a friend pointed me towards an ecumenical online conference on disability. I was hoping that I might listen to some interesting ideas in a "head" kind of way but was utterly unprepared that it would prompt a profound experience in my heart. At the beginning we were put into small breakout groups to introduce ourselves, which we did in turn. Naturally enough I was asked if I had any direct experience of disability. I mumbled something about being dyspraxic at which the others broke into a round of applause and cheered.

I'd never had this reaction before. I'd come to think of my dyspraxia as something to be managed and to be hidden if possible. At school when I needed to go to the special educational needs teachers, my classmates would put their tongues in their lower lips and call me "speshal" and "spaz". But here, I experienced feeling not just included, or tolerated, or adapted to, but celebrated and given permission to turn up as my full self. Not feeling I needed to be "fixed" was a profound relief. I might even call it healing. In the first break I had a little cry.

A social view of disability understands that rather than being inherently disabled, people are often dis-abled by society. Today perhaps we could consider, for example, a lack of wheelchair ramps or reasonable adjustments a kind of structural, societal sin. Perhaps when Jesus "casts out sin" he is referring to the structural, societal sin of inequality that disables people.

There's weight to this view in how people react. When Jesus makes what seems impossible happen, he is not asked "how on earth did you do that?" which would surely be the first question if someone did a healing miracle today. Instead, he is asked "who gave you the authority to do this?" The same is later asked to Jesus' friend Peter when he accompanies a disabled man into a part of the Temple from which he has been excluded. Many activists today will recognise the question "who gave you the authority?" as the words of those who prefer order to justice.

A similar case can be made with relation to mental health. Poor mental health can arise from the contradictions of colonial and post-colonial societies. Could we see Jesus saying this too? In one of the more cryptic miracles Jesus "casts evil spirits" from an unwell man named "Legion" into a herd of pigs. A legion is a division of Roman soldiers, and pigs in Jewish culture are unclean. The pigs then charge into the sea of Galilee, like the army being expelled from Judea. I read him as saying that social conditions must be changed in order for more people to enjoy better mental health.

Changing societal structures is hard and involves making arguments that defy accepted wisdom as well as challenging authority. But the task of the person committed to significant change is to make what at one time seemed impossible, become in hindsight inevitable. In other words, we're attempting something not far short of a miracle. Faith – including the faith that change is possible – can sustain us to commit the time and effort that this level of change requires of us.

As we do so we might remember that some of the Bible's principal characters may well have had various impairments too. Isaac is depicted as blind. In some translations Moses is described as having a speech impediment. Jesus after the resurrection still has holes in his wrists, legs and side – the risen Christ is wounded. But most of all God is described in Ezekiel and Daniel as having a throne with wheels.

As equality and inclusion advocate Becky Tyler puts it: "In fact it's not just any old chair, it's the best chair in the Bible. It's God's throne, and it's a wheelchair. This made me feel like God understands what it's like to have a wheelchair and that having a wheelchair is actually very cool, because God has one."

## Gender equality

The Christian church has a lot to atone for when it comes to the treatment of women. Rather than being a counterbalance to the violence of patriarchy, the church has too often ignored, upheld or practised it. Roman Emperor Constantine, who made Christianity the faith of his empire, killed his wife. King Henry VIII who made himself head of a new English church after breaking with Rome, killed two of his wives. There are still Christian churches where women are denied a voice and where safeguards against sexual abuse have failed.

There's no escaping that the Bible has been used to entrench gender inequality. Very often it centres the stories of men – a problem deepened by the men who translated it, interpreted it and preached about it. There are even questions about what was included. Some of the mystical "Gnostic" texts that were left out of the Bible, describe a divine feminine wisdom (Greek: *Sophia*) and in the Gospel of Mary Magdalene we learn more about Jesus' best-known female disciple. The Apocryphon of John depicts an androgynous God who declares "I am the father, I am the mother". In the Gospel of Thomas, Peter is called out for a disparaging sexist comment.

Even within the works that were included in the official versions there is a theme of women's equality. In the opening story, God puts enmity between women and the serpent. Among the prophets is Jeremiah who speaks of a day when gender relations would be different. When co-founder of Quakerism and foremother of Christian feminism Margaret Fell read these texts, she declared that day had come.

The New Testament mentions many female leaders. The most famous is Mary Magdalene, another is named Susanna and another Joanna who is the wife of the client king's head servant. In neighbouring Samaria, the movement is built by a woman. The female disciples are there at the crucifixion even when most of the men have scarpered. Women are also the first witnesses to the resurrection. The Book of Acts describes the Light of Christ being poured on all men and all women and through the Letters of Paul we know of numerous women who hosted and led early church meetings. The very final book describes a new Jerusalem, depicted as a woman.

All this is consistent with what Jesus teaches. When he speaks of the Kingdom of Heaven/Kingdom of God, he says it would be like a group of young women who go in first to a banquet, like a woman who loses a coin and then finds it and like a woman mixing yeast into dough.

When he sees rich men making extravagant donations to the Temple followed by a poorer woman who puts in just two coins, Jesus turns to his students and tells them that the woman put in proportionately more. When a woman rumoured to be a sex worker approaches Jesus, the men around him hope he will send her away. Instead, Jesus defies societal conventions and affirms her.

On another occasion a group of men interrupts as Jesus is teaching a lecture. They bring with them a woman accused of having an affair and demand to know whether Jesus thinks that she should be killed. He turns around and suggests "let him without sin cast the first stone".

In this quick turn of phrase Jesus echoes Isaiah by shining a light on the systemic sin of patriarchy. Why was the man in the affair not being so treated? What about the affairs the men themselves might have had? Wasn't it in turn sinful for the woman to be treated as she was? The term "male fragility" might not be out of place to describe the men's response. They walk out, leaving the woman behind.

It does well to ask more of the woman in this story. Had she had an abortion? Was it her idea that they all go to Jesus as a means of saving her life, as he would make the point she had been making all along, but they were so sexist they'd only hear it from a man? Finding unanswered questions and gaps in the Bible can help us to ask whose perspectives need listening to today. When Christians organise protests outside abortion clinics, we might well encourage those people to meditate on the questions posed by this story.

Yet for all this, the Bible is set in a patriarchal culture, and those attitudes shape the actions of the characters. How do we read those in the light of Jesus' teaching? One answer to this is offered by Esther Mombo who describes women's groups in Kenya exploring instances of sexism in the Bible as a means to analyse the contemporary sexism they face. She Concludes: "the Bible as such is not an instrument of oppression of women, so much as a lopsided interpretation of the Bible, vested with ulterior motives."

For years the church has taught this lopsided interpretation, but at last the tide is turning. To quote ground-breaking Bible scholar Marcella Althaus-Reid, feminist readings offer an "authentic Christian conversion, a turning away from the structures of patriarchal sin". There are some who act to keep things the way they used to be, believing this is the way to be "respectable".

But the true manifestation of respect is equality and removing the barriers that have held people back.

## Anti-racism

As I write, one of the movements setting agendas and making change is Black Lives Matter. Originating in the US, protesting police killing Black people, the movement calls on all institutions to examine the ways in which they perpetuate racism. Both the US and UK governments are pushing back. But other groups are having long overdue conversations, including white-majority churches where the structural sin of racism – including as perpetuated by churches – is at last being widely discussed.

The notion of race is only a few hundred years old. Uncomfortably for Christians, the system of categorising people as "white" and "Black" emerged out of colonial Christian supremacist ideas that were used to justify enslaving non-Christians. When enslaved people began attending Christian gatherings, a new system of inequality was invented to preserve the violence of the existing social order. It was the basis of white supremacy.

White Christianity has often depicted Jesus and the disciples as pale skinned. Given they were what we now call Middle Eastern, this is unlikely to say the least. The people in the New Testament most likely to have been "white" are the Roman occupiers. Even then it's worth remembering that the lower ranks of the Roman army were much more ethnically diverse than white history often chooses to remember.

Race, though, is not biological, but a social system about power. In this respect the Bible shows systems of inequality which are too familiar: Darker skinned peoples in large parts of what we now call North Africa and the Middle East suffering under the weight of an empire controlled by lighter-skinned people of European descent. We also find examples in the Bible of societal prejudice against migrants. In contrast, Jesus – himself once a refugee – teaches unity, encapsulated in what is probably his most famous parable.

It begins when a lawyer enquires which is the most important law. Jesus replies that "Love God and love your neighbour" sums up all the others. "But who is my neighbour?" the lawyer follows up. Jesus responds with a story about a man who was robbed and left for dead by the side of the road. First a powerful priest, then another religious man pass along the road, but hurry by without stopping to help. It is only the third passer-by – a migrant from Samaria – who helps the injured person. Jesus asks the lawyer who is the neighbour in this story. "The one who stopped to help," the lawyer replies as if unable say "it was the migrant".

In the Acts of the Apostles, we learn that the movement that emerged after Jesus' crucifixion includes people who had been born in the places known today as Iran, Iraq, Turkey, Egypt Libya and the Occupied Palestinian Territories. Soon afterwards what is now Syria becomes a centre for the movement. The first non-Jewish person to join the movement is a eunuch from Ethiopia who works in what is now Sudan. As I write out the modern names of these places, it weighs upon me how my own notionally "Christian" country treats people from these places. The only time I have been among this diversity of people was in the refugee camp in Calais.

There is one person in the Jesus movement who we can be pretty sure was "white": his name is Cornelius, a Roman soldier of the Italian regiment, who to everyone's surprise asks to join the movement. No one seems to have worried when the first non-Jew joined – the Ethiopian eunuch worked for the Kingdom of Kush which did not oppress the Hebrew people and indeed had been a historic opponent of the Roman Empire. In contrast the prospect of an oppressor joining leads to an almighty row, which in different forms continues through the Book of Acts as the movement spreads west.

In the end it is agreed that such people do have a place under certain conditions; after all the spirit had been poured out on all people. Even Jesus praised the faith of a Roman centurion. But white readers would do well to read this with humility. Christianity's beginnings are in what might today be called a Black, Indigenous and People of Colour-led movement to which people of European descent were only a later addition. As some must have feared from the start, white Christianity has often acted much more like the Roman Empire than it has like the Kingdom of Heaven.

Perhaps this is most starkly the case when we consider the cross and compare it to the lynching tree, which in turn has so many parallels with modern forms of state violence against Black people. As James Cone makes clear: "Both were public spectacles, shameful events, instruments of punishment reserved for the most despised people in society."

Cone didn't live to see the global reaction to the killing of

George Floyd, but his words have gained a new life among Christians concerned for racism: "until we can see the cross and the lynching tree together, until we can identify Christ with a 're-crucified' Black body hanging from a lynching tree, there can be no genuine understanding of Christian identity in America, and no deliverance from the brutal legacy of slavery and white supremacy."

## Class

For as long as there has been "civilisation" there have been systems of class inequality. Many in working-class movements have concurred with the view that the history of society is the history of struggle between oppressor and oppressed.

In the system we read about in the Gospels there's little doubt as to where Jesus is positioned. He works as a carpenter, as does Joseph, possibly as a low paid day-labourer on Herodian construction sites. His mother, Mary, describes herself as a servant-girl. Later in life Jesus describes himself as having been hungry, thirsty and in need of clothes and declares himself as one with all people who experience this.

His closest friends are employed in what could be thought of as working-class occupations. The first recruits to Jesus' team are fishermen who lack formal education. Matthew is something akin to a bailiff, collecting taxes to be sent back to Rome. Like Jesus' mother, Joanna is part of a servant family, albeit one earning enough to donate some money to the movement. Others of those he associates with, such as Mary of Bethany, are rumoured to be engaged in sex work.

It's notable that while Jesus critiques the system, like John he doesn't blame working-class people caught up in it for the jobs that they do. He declares that sex workers and tax collectors would enter the Kingdom of God long before rich lawyers and priests. Also like John, he describes the rich and powerful as a "brood of vipers" who are "full of greed and self-indulgence".

When a lawyer interrupts him to say he is offended, Jesus rebuffs him as a hypocrite who speaks highly of the reformers of the past even whilst persecuting those who try to change things today.

This is not an isolated outburst. On another occasion after speaking of hope for the dispossessed, Jesus condemns the rich and the greedy. When a rich man asks to join the movement, Jesus tells him to sell all he owns and give it to the poor. When he doesn't, he tells his followers that it's easier for a camel to pass through the eye of a needle than it is for a rich man to enter the Kingdom of God.

This is in keeping with his stories of what the Kingdom is like: labourers earning an equal wage, people's debts being cancelled, and the first being last and the last being first. In the light of such a vision, the words "your Kingdom come" in what we call the Lord's Prayer, have radical implications and "forgive us our debts as we forgive our debtors" a call to an economic reset, a jubilee of debt cancellation, and a viable route to much greater equality.

There's also a realistic assessment of how difficult winning this change will be. One of Jesus' last parables tells of a servant who stands up to his boss and refuses to be complicit in making unearned wealth for his cruel master, for which he is thrown out into obscurity. As anyone who has challenged unjust power knows: the system does not reward those who challenge it.

One of those who resisted who has been cast into obscurity by church tradition is Jesus' brother James, the first Bishop of Jerusalem. The book that carries his name – possibly a transcription of a sermon (or sermons) he made – contains a direct challenge to wealth and power, in the tradition of the prophets: "Your riches have rotted and your garments are moth-eaten. Your gold and silver have corroded, and their corrosion will be evidence against you"; "the wages of the laborers who mowed your fields, which you kept back by fraud, are crying out against you"; "the rich will fade away".

He explains true religion means "refusing to let the world corrupt you" and that "faith is dead without good works". To communities who perpetuate inequality by giving a good seat to rich visitors while telling poor visitors to sit on the floor, he asks a series of rhetorical questions: "doesn't this show your judgments are led by evil motives? Hasn't God chosen the poor to inherit the Kingdom? Isn't it the rich who oppress and slander you?"

The movement in Jerusalem that followed James was called the Ebionites which translates as "the poor", the inception of which is unknown. This raises some tantalising possibilities. When Jesus says "blessed are the poor" could he be talking about a pre-existing movement started by John the Baptist? When he suggests the rich man gives all his money to "the poor" did he mean he should donate it to the struggle? And when James says "the poor" will inherit the Kingdom is he making a revolutionary declaration?

In this light it is worth thinking back to Jesus' most famous miracle, remembering that all of his actions have a message. When the disciples have only a few fish and loaves of bread to share around a whole crowd, Jesus asks that it be shared equally. We could call it a nonviolent "propaganda of the deed". A prefigurative act of redistribution. Whether through others doing likewise or divine intervention (and perhaps the two are not as different as they sound) everyone has enough to eat.

But the masses needed more than bread. They were hungry and thirsty for justice. As John would later write, "let us not love in word or in tongue, but in deed". Jesus was often asked when the great change would come. "That day or hour no one knows," he replied. When again he was pressed for more detail he revealed "the Kingdom of God is already among you". The time to bring the message to the capital was drawing closer.

## LGBTQIA+ equality

At this point it's worth pausing to consider what Jesus did not say. Those whose ideas about Christianity have been shaped by wealthy men preaching homophobia may be surprised that while Jesus said a great deal about critiquing the rich and powerful, he did not speak against homosexuality once.

What he does talk about, many times and at length, is love, in particular to "love your neighbour as yourself". We can read this as exhortation to be kind and do justice, but the implications are much deeper and wider. Love can also be a physical act. Loving others as ourselves not only encompasses but can be seen to describe, loving people of the same sex or gender.

As sexual diversity exists within all societies, it's likely that a significant number of the 3000-plus people mentioned in the Bible, were not what we might think of as "straight". In the Hebrew scriptures it's been suggested that Adam – born of the earth – could be thought of as the first nonbinary human being. Joseph (of Technicolour Dreamcoat fame) could be read as having worn a dress, in rejection of binary gender roles. Others have noted the fierce same-sex love between Ruth and Naomi and between Jonathan and David. The Song of Songs can be read as a gay love poem.

Some of the most astonishing questions asked refer to Jesus directly, for example, asking who was the man who at the time of Jesus' arrest ran towards the soldiers naked except for a sheet? Was he the same as or different from the "disciple Jesus loved" referenced as present at the crucifixion? And what about Mary Magdalene – were she and Jesus ever anything more than "just good friends"? Others have enquired what Jesus' sex would have been if he was born with the absence of male DNA.

Some trans Christians note the ways that Jesus' body changes as the story progresses, notably in the episode known as the transfiguration. On that day, in the presence of a few close friends, Jesus ascends a hill. In the process he becomes something more indeterminate and universal than a man. In the death and resurrection that follows, some have found a metaphor for the rebirth people can experience in transitioning gender. From these and other questions, scholars have theorised that Jesus could have been nonbinary, genderqueer, intersex, asexual, homosexual, bisexual, pansexual, genderqueer or indeed straight, and in this possibly changing through the course of his life. For myself I view Jesus as transcending such classifications, but as I do so, I am reminded that gender and sexuality are by no means binary, straightforward or easily organised into rigid categories.

What is clear is that Jesus doesn't discriminate. When a Roman centurion asks in marketplace Greek for Jesus to help his servant, he could be understood to be asking Jesus to help his same-sex partner, as the word for "servant" has an ambiguous meaning. But Jesus doesn't stop to ask, he simply helps, and praises the brave risk the centurion has taken.

Another affirmation of sexual diversity can be found in Jesus' instruction to his friends not to be prejudiced against eunuchs. The word eunuch refers to a person whose genitalia has been altered, and the antiquated term for an intersex person ("congenital eunuch") refers to people who are born with genitals which do not fit binary notions of sex. In the ancient world eunuchs were often associated with homosexuality or indeed asexuality. Bible scholar Peterson Toscano reads eunuchs as among the queer people of the day. One way or another it's fair to say eunuchs would be covered by the initialism LGBTQIA+. Presumably the apostles take on Jesus' belief in equality, as the first non-Jewish person to join the movement is a eunuch.

Jesus finishes his exhortation not to discriminate by declaring "The one who can accept this should accept it." Why did he feel the need to add this when he's already made himself so clear? To my mind, I hear a first-century precedent to the great Stonewall campaign messages of recent times: "Some people are gay, some people are trans, get over it!"

## Protest

Part of the life of those who want change involves attending and sometimes organising public demonstrations. Even when thousands amass on the streets, these seldom win the change called for straight away. They do, however, demonstrate the depth and breadth of feeling of the many people who want change. In many countries such protests are outlawed or suppressed, leaving activists with dilemmas about whether or when to engage in actions that could lead to arrest. So it was in first-century Jerusalem.

We pick up the story: the movement decides to take their message to the capital during the festival of Passover, perhaps assessing that the crowds present from the places they have been organising in would mean a maximum number of sympathetic people present and a higher level of protection. They start forming up outside of the city walls then begin their procession to the gate. Jesus joins on the back of a donkey, contrasting himself as a man of the people, to the pageantry of armies and kings on horseback. As they go their numbers grow. By the time they reach the city, people are packed through the streets, chanting "hosanna" which roughly translates as "liberate us".

More and more join as the demonstration winds round to the great building at the centre of the city. I imagine the mixed feelings of the movement looking upon the Temple – on one hand an awe-inspiring building thought of as the holiest place in the world, on the other hand a symbol of compromise and collaboration with Roman rule. When they arrive at the location for the rally, they find it filled with people selling animals for sacrifice and trading currency. With a deep breath Jesus goes about overturning the tables, freeing doves from their cages and rescuing the cows from an early death. Then the crowds occupy the space, symbolically reclaiming the Temple.

When Jesus rises to speak, he does not mince his words. He calls the people in power hypocrites who should resign. An emergency security meeting is called to decide how to deal with the troublemaker in their midst but they choose not to arrest him in public for fear that there would be a riot. But once he leaves the Temple they don't know his whereabouts. Here Jesus' friend Judas gains a larger part in the story. He reveals Jesus' hideout to the authorities. Why he does so remains an open question. Was he just an untrustworthy person, motivated only by monetary reward? Or did he believe that Jesus' arrest would trigger the uprising that would lead to the Kingdom of Heaven? Some of those present get word to Jesus warning him he is at risk. But Jesus knows he can't stop now. He needs to see this through to the end.

The friends gather to eat in a concealed room where Jesus washes the feet of each of those present. They share a simple meal during which Jesus reveals that he knows he's been betrayed. As they continue, Jesus says there could be no greater love than to give one's life for others and exhorts them to love one another as he had loved them. With this he says he has taught all he knows. After dinner they take a walk. Then, just as predicted, the authorities come and seize Jesus to arrest him. As the soldiers advance towards him Jesus tries to calm the situation, but the disciples scatter, except for a man dressed only in a sheet. When the soldiers try to seize him, he escapes entirely naked.

Jesus does not resist, but says he knows it is his destiny, and is led by the soldiers to the cells.

## Prisoner of conscience

In the early 1960s Peter Benenson, a lawyer and recent convert to Catholicism, was reading the newspaper on the London Underground. Finding an article about some people arrested for expressing their opinions, he found his way to a church, St Martin-in-the-Fields near Trafalgar Square. There he realised that he had to do something about it, and with his friend Eric Baker – a peace campaigner and former conscientious objector who had himself risked jail for his beliefs – co-founded Amnesty International to work for the fulfilment of all people's human rights, beginning by campaigning against torture, against the death penalty and for freedom for political prisoners.

When half a century later I started work for the same organisation, I became interested in its "origin story". I followed in Benenson's footsteps, to the same church in London, and sat down in a pew, looking up at the cross at the front. What was it that happened to him in that moment? Should I understand it as merely a secular experience arising from having found a quiet place to think or did something more spiritual happen?

Crucifixion was a brutal punishment under the Roman Empire, reserved for people who challenged authority, especially enslaved people who rose up against their masters. If it happened today, we'd call Jesus a Human Rights Defender, who became a prisoner of conscience for exercising his freedom of expression and assembly. We'd emphasise his nonviolence and we'd likely send observers to his trial. In first-century Judea that would have been harder, but Benenson's namesake, Peter friend of Jesus, did what he could.

In the story, Peter begins by following Jesus to the courts. This is dangerous work. A woman at the gate listens to his accent and looks into his face (was she looking at his skin colour?) and interrogates him as to his identity. But Peter stands his ground and manages to stay where he is, even while feeling inward shame for denying his friend. But while the protection of the crowd had been enough to delay Jesus' arrest, it wouldn't be enough to save his earthly life.

What follows could not be described as a fair trial. A gathering of politically powerful people spends little time in deciding to hand Jesus to the Roman authorities. For the most part Jesus gives a "no-comment interview". Asked if he is going to defend himself, he doesn't reply, perhaps unwilling to give the biased process any legitimacy. Asked if he claims to be the King of the Jews he replies "that is what you say". Only when he is asked if he is the one who fulfilled the prophesy, does he take a deep breath and say "I am". The high priest flies into a rage and calls for him to be executed. The people in the courtroom spit in his face, slap him and hit him, before throwing him to the guards who beat him still more. Human rights laws are supposed to protect people from cruel and degrading treatment. But there was no such protection for Jesus. The guards put a crown of painful thorns on his head and then mocked him by bowing down and declaring "all hail the king" before hitting him with sticks, spitting at him, then stripping him again.

To the authorities he was no doubt just one in a long line of political prisoners. Elsewhere the Bible mentions Judas the Galilean and another protester called Theudas. Due for crucifixion alongside Jesus were two other rebels – the punishment of death on a cross was reserved for those who resisted authority. There was also Barabbas, a revolutionary described as having incited riots in the capital.

Perhaps to give the masses the illusion of choice without disrupting the structures of power, the authorities allow the populace to decide whether to execute Barabbas or Jesus, in something akin to a referendum. But Barabbas is local, and perhaps his methods are more understandable. The crowd calls for Barabbas' release.

Jesus is forced to march through the city, carrying the instrument of his torture on his back. When they reach a mountaintop, nails are driven through Jesus' wrists and into a plank of wood, which is lifted on another piece of wood for all to see. His feet are nailed into place and a spear is driven into his side. Above his head is nailed the charge against him. People come to mock him and demand he perform miracles. One of the rebels hung to the side of him yells insults. The other acts in the spirit of solidarity requesting "Jesus, remember me when you come into your Kingdom".

Around noon the sky darkens, the air falls cold and a chill wind blows. Jesus prays out loud one last time the 22nd psalm: "My God, my God, why have you forsaken me?" But he gets no further than the very first line. Then he breathes his last.

Today when I think of Peter Benenson looking up at the cross at St Martin's, I think of the abuses that are still happening: the suppression of the freedom of expression and assembly, wrongful imprisonment, torture and the death penalty. I think of people in poverty and suffering from environmental destruction. I think of people who have been killed by the police, or who have not been protected from hate crimes. And I remember that still today, people die because of our sins, just as Jesus did.

# Chapter 3

# The activism of the apostles

## The struggle continues

Part of my growth as a campaigner for change has been learning about losing. On occasion, I have all but collapsed, disappointed, distraught, close to disconsolate, when efforts to change things haven't been enough to affect the structures that uphold injustice.

But how much worse it must have been for Jesus' closest friends. The person who had led and taught them, with whom they shared in the "eternal life" and for whom they had risked so much, had been killed, and before long the authorities would be after them too.

It is the women who first work out that Jesus' death isn't the end. They return to the men to explain this realisation, but the men are too consumed with mourning to listen. A few days later, the men go for a hike where they are joined by a stranger. They open their hearts to him, sharing their devastation at what has happened. Only later do they realise that the stranger is Jesus.

They feel a growing peace within themselves. As it grows, they see someone before them who looks like their teacher, but who appears simultaneously both ghostly and yet also entirely real. Slowly it dawns on them that the personification of love is winning out after all by returning to life and reassuring the disorientated group, encouraging them to help others to know this peace too.

From that point on they wait in their safe-houses and hiding places, until one day the weather turns and wind fills the draughty houses. In the house where the leadership are staying something happens inwardly to all of the group at once and they find themselves shouting out with joy. Their stress and grief lift and their hearts fill with relief. They shout so loud that they attract a crowd who ask if they are drunk. But they respond explaining what they all realise. The loving spirit of Christ is still with them.

Long is the list of those who have resisted authority, whose lives were brutally cut short. In modern times we might name Joe Hill, Mohandas Gandhi, Martin Luther King Jr, Fred Hampton, Ruth First, Steve Biko, Ken Saro-Wiwa, Oscar Romero, Chico Mendes and Berta Cáceres, to name just ten. Affirmations of the struggle continuing after the death of leaders are manifested in slogans: "Don't mourn, organise", "You can kill the revolutionary but not the revolution", "she is a seed that has multiplied".

When I read about Jesus' friends resolving to continue the movement, I hear the words "La Lucha Continua" in my mind. There's no doubt that their decision is personally risky, but perhaps that's what Jesus meant when he had asked them "to pick up your cross and follow me". They pick themselves up, take stock of what they are against, and they carry on, reassured by a radical realisation: the spirit of the loving liberator they had known, can be known by anyone in their hearts, and the Kingdom can be built by anyone who acts on it.

## Peter

Trying to follow Jesus' example is hard. How can we even try to emulate someone so profoundly good? If there's any consolation, in the Bible we read that even Jesus' closest friends often fall short of what is needed of them, but Jesus loves them nevertheless.

A few weeks beforehand, Jesus had appointed Peter to be his successor telling him he would be the rock upon which the community would grow. Peter had soon started telling the others what to do – even Jesus. At that point Jesus had sighed and told Peter he might be more of a stumbling block. Then he looked to the others and said that if anyone put themselves before others, they would only end up selling out. Peter did all he could to live up to the role assigned to him. During the last supper before Jesus' arrest, Jesus had said that Peter would deny him three times before the following morning. Peter promised he never would. Yet it was exactly as Jesus had said. As if trying to prove himself and the leadership role bestowed upon him, when the guards had come for Jesus, Peter had drawn his sword, ready to kill those who had come, despite Jesus' teaching against violence. But Jesus ordered Peter to put down his sword, adding that those who live by the sword, die by it too.

For weeks after Jesus' crucifixion his friends wait, directionless. After the realisation that the Holy Spirit is with them, however, they get active, following the leadings of the spirit. Firstly, as Jesus had said, they sell their property and share the money, from each according to their ability to each according to their need. They also start rebuilding the movement, meeting by night in one another's houses, and calling open air public meetings in the city centre by day.

This is an audacious move for which the authorities arrest the entire committee and imprison them. But during the night, they escape and return to where they had been arrested to continue spreading the word, where they are re-arrested and taken directly to the courtroom. Although the guards would have dearly liked to have beaten the protesters, they fear for what the public reaction would be. In the end, to their surprise, the arrestees escape the death penalty, following the intervention of Gamaliel, a respected lawyer. Instead they are whipped, then set free.

The movement celebrates their return, but it soon becomes clear that while their attention had been elsewhere, problems have begun to occur with the distribution of food. In particular it emerges that women from some ethnic groups are being made to wait longer than others. The leadership are shocked when they hear this, but realise that they must take the blame, as it was them who had responsibility for distributing food, and who therefore should be accountable.

So they call the community together to hear the leaders' apology and to propose that a new group should be added to the leadership with the sole responsibility for ensuring that food is distributed fairly. Their suggestion is met with warmth by the assembly, and seven more are nominated, the first of whom is named Stephen.

One of my favourite Quaker advices is "think it possible that you may be mistaken". For spiritual growth, scientific progress or collective social change the most certain of us need to hold open the possibility that we haven't got it right. Even Peter, Jesus' closest friend, was capable of interpreting or acting on things in ways that fell short, both during and after the earthly life of Jesus.

But in these texts, we also find some hints for how to organise in the context of this recognition. The early church practised collective and distributed leadership. They helped even out inequalities of power by taking action to even out inequalities of wealth. And when the leaders let something slip, they owned up to their mistakes to the community at large, and came up with a system to prevent it recurring. Many leaders today could learn from that.

## Paul

For many years I pretty much dismissed Paul. Many of the New Testament passages wielded to hurt and harm those with less power are drawn from his words. When we first meet him (at that stage named Saul) he is overseeing the execution of Stephen, after which he starts to round up other leaders in Jerusalem. Then he travels to Damascus to keep hunting down the movement there.

On the way, though, he has an out of body experience. He encounters Jesus' spirit on the road who asks why it is that Saul is persecuting him. He changes his mind and on arrival announces his defection to the movement. He begins to reflect and travels to Mount Sanai in Arabia, possibly as a form of pilgrimage. He becomes a tentmaker and travelling teacher, and eventually changes his name to Paul, which means "small" or "humble".

Most of the rest of the New Testament consists of his letters, addressed to the emerging Christian communities of the time. At first read some of his teaching seems to contradict that of Jesus, and at times he even seems to contradict himself. It's easy to conclude that for all he thought he'd changed, he didn't leave all his old ways behind. But that conclusion is too easy. Aware that my approach to reading wasn't leading to an interpretation that leads to charity, I delved into some of the scholarship on Paul. There is a considerable amount of enquiry about who authored which of the texts. It's thought that some of the letters were written by others, with consensus about only seven of the books coming from Paul directly. Instead of reading his letters in the order they are presented in the Bible (broadly speaking from the longest to the shortest), I tried reading them in the order they were thought to have been written: 1 Thessalonians, Galatians, 1 Corinthians, 2 Corinthians, Philemon, Philippians and Romans.

Through this process a very different picture emerges: not of someone who changes completely on the road to Damascus but who throughout his life is on a spiritual journey, from the zeal of his early life through the self-assuredness and certainty of the recent convert, towards humility and nuance based on his experience at the end. His style shifts from one of confrontation, towards encouraging an approach based on reconciliation and acceptance of difference.

Paul has moments where he is more and less self-aware. In his early letter to the Galatians, he lists his achievements in a way that suggests he is feeling defensive and hurt. In the same letter he appears to "lash out" and calls the non-Roman community in colonised Judea the children of slaves (and therefore wrong) – an insensitive choice of words to say the least. By the time of his letters to the movement in Corinth he admits that he sees things only "imperfectly, like puzzling reflections in a mirror" and that "in this self-confident boasting I am not talking as the Lord would, but as a fool." By the time of his final letter, he refers to himself as "all too human" and "a slave to sin".

Yet for all that his words have been abused by oppressors, it's very clear that Paul is on the side of the oppressed, and suffers not only for the content of his teaching but the ways in which he too is marginalised. He is arrested, imprisoned and tried many times – persecuted by the slaveowners and wealthy businessmen whose privilege he disrupts. These same people display what we'd now call antisemitism, as they use Paul's Judaism against him. Paul's inner turmoil must have grown all the more when he is accused by some in his own community of not being Jewish enough.

In Athens home to the Temple of Nike and the Hill of Mars he is put on trial for condemning their gods as idols. A recent biographer of Paul reflects that his condemnation of idols "must have seemed unrealistic. One might as well stand in the middle of Wall Street and declare that the entire banking system is a category mistake". But in recent years people have done something very like that – in 2011 there were protest camps, for months on end, under the banner *Occupy Wall Street* which then spread to financial districts around the world. In the tentmaker Paul there is a first-century forebear.

In contrast to how he is often depicted, Paul affirms gender equality through his actions, including celebrating very many female church leaders, especially Priscilla who he mentions several times in his letters. In his first letter to the Corinthians, he makes it clear that women and men do and should speak in church. A contradictory passage in the same letter saying the opposite is thought to have been added after Paul's death in the course of a controversy about women's participation. He speaks of the presence of a universal love – a love so strong that it transcends inherited customs, rules, and even socially constructed identities – an experience shared by many queer Christians. In modern times Paul himself would fall into the LGBTQIA+ initialism. Today he is celebrated as an early asexual, based on a line in a letter to the movement in Corinth in which he calls his single status a gift from God. At that point he implied that any sexual activity at all is inferior to celibacy. By the time of his final letter, to the church in Rome, he refers to various consensual sexual acts taking place and asks people not to judge, but to love.

Yet for all the ways he himself is marginalised, Paul never really faces up to the unearned power and privilege that he bears as a citizen of the Roman Empire, which saves his life several times, provides him better treatment in custody and on one occasion even prompts an apology from the authorities. We may well interpret some of his angrier moments as flowing from the fragility and injured pride of the privileged. But we can also observe that, incomplete as his perspective inevitably is, he does what he can. Paul is always a "work in progress". Even in his imperfection, God has a purpose for him.

As a relatively privileged white man reading the Bible today, I'm challenged by Paul. Are there times when I too am insensitive or unaware of the consequences of my actions, especially on people who are less powerful than me? It's likely that despite my efforts I perpetuate the structural sins I benefit from, and some unjust societal prejudices will have seeped into me. I too am "all too human".

In Paul I find not a faultless saint, but someone who

represents the challenges of trying to simultaneously live in and transform a system that is imbued with injustice. In his letters I encounter a conviction and determination to change the world that I admire, and a mirror of some of the characteristics in myself that I work every day to transform.

## Resilience

For those who have hoped to see a great change and had those hopes dashed, one of the greatest challenges of work for social change is just coping, "staying afloat", building resilience and continuing in the face of adversity. I don't think any of us really manages it all the time, God knows I don't. Neither does Paul who describes himself and his companions as feeling "crushed and overwhelmed, beyond our ability to endure", and like "fragile clay jars" against the weight of the world. Haven't we all sometimes felt something like that?

But some people, then and now, develop strategies to help them stay in the struggle for the long haul. It's striking how much of the letters speak to this theme and prefigure some of the secular support offered today.

In his first letter, Peter writes of the trials of the movement but asks them to be glad and think of their temporary troubles like fire which purifies gold. James echoes this: "when troubles come your way, consider it an opportunity for great joy ... when your endurance is complete you will be perfect". Paul too: "Live clean, innocent lives as children of God, shining like bright lights in a world full of crooked and perverse people." Did Rebecca Solnit have any of this in her mind when she suggested in her classic book *Hope in the Dark* that activists "make yourself one small republic of unconquered spirit"?

Another person supporting activists experiencing burnout today is Laura van Dernoot Lipsky. In her view, sustaining ourselves in the long term requires us to nurture a deep well of reserves she describes as "an open space in which we are being moved instead of moving". Among other things, this helps us cope with the decreased quality of decisions we make when we have to make them at speed over time. Hold that in mind when we read of Paul praying that "your love may overflow more and more with knowledge and full insight to help you determine what is best".

Indeed, there is a lot of modern sounding advice in there. Where today we might be advised to think of something to be thankful for every night and every morning, Paul advises "Tell God what you need and thank him for all he has done. Then you will experience God's peace". Where today we know that spending time in nature, appreciating art, laughing, meditating and doing the things we feel passionately about are all good for us, there it is in Paul too: "Fix your thoughts on what is true and honourable, and right and pure and lovely and admirable. Think about things that are excellent and worthy of praise ... then the God of peace will be with you".

Humility is good for us when it helps us be curious rather than angry when we encounter an opposing view, and better able to stay calm when engaging with it. The letter to the Philippians, written from prison, marks something of a turning point in Paul's style, and advises "in humility regard others as better than yourselves". We also learn that Paul's incarceration has actually helped build the movement as it means people are talking about it. This reminds us that sometimes the results of our work appear slowly, or even seem opposite to what we hoped, but often there can be benefits we only sometimes see. Even from the prison cell there can be grounds for hope.

Behind bars, Paul meditates and prays and seems to reach some kind of wellbeing, writing: "I have learnt how to be content with whatever I have. I know how to live on almost nothing or with everything." Could he have reached the same insight taught by Buddhists that attachment (sometimes translated as acquisition) is the root of all suffering? Buddhism also teaches something of the liberation of impermanence. How fascinating to find something similar in the letter of James: "your life is like the morning fog ... it is here a little while and then it is gone".

Those first-century writers hoped to see the Kingdom of Heaven in their lifetimes, and had to adapt when it didn't seem to come so soon. But then, remember Jesus' mysterious words: even under the Roman Empire that killed him "the Kingdom of Heaven is already among you". Later Paul declares "we are citizens of heaven". And again, I hear this echoed in Rebecca Solnit's twenty-first-century advice: "When activists mistake heaven for some goal at which they must arrive rather than an idea to navigate by, they burn themselves out".

And so, they set about building the new society in the shell of the old one (Peter calls it being a "peculiar people"). James talks about reducing tension in the community – praying instead of judging one another and instead of quarrelling. Paul implores the movement in Rome not to conform any longer to the patterns of this world, but to renew their minds and their communities, anticipating the change that must come by loving one another and their neighbours, and supporting one another in the struggle.

## The Book of Revolution

Dreams sometimes tell us more than we realise. I remember when I started working in partnership with an organisation that I had reservations about I dreamed I was a snake-charmer who was bitten by one of the snakes. Another time, when I was asked to work on a campaign that I thought didn't tackle the root causes of the issue, I dreamt I was being congratulated for wafting some fruit flies out of the window of a building that was falling down. Dreams have long formed a part of how societies have understood themselves. So it was in biblical times. It's possible that the last book of the Bible is not literally an account of a dream but a work of apocalyptic literature written to support the communities struggling under the weight of empire, told through the device of a dream. The word *apocalypsis* means "to reveal" – like drawing back a curtain and looking through, hence the title "Revelation". The question is, what is it that it reveals?

I find it helpful to try and imagine what could have been in the mind of the author. Peter and Paul had been executed by Roman Emperor Nero in the wake of the great fire of Rome for which Christians had been made scapegoats. James had been stoned to death on the Temple Mount. In 66 CE there had been an uprising against the empire in Jerusalem. But it was defeated and the city was looted and left in ruins. Those people who did not escape the city were massacred or enslaved, including what remained of the Jerusalem church. John sought sanctuary on a Greek island. He may have been suffering PTSD. The empire appeared to have won. The Temple had been destroyed and replaced with a symbol of Roman authority and imperial worship. Even in Asia where the movement lived on, demands were being made of the community to worship the symbols of empire. Against this background the book tells us that John had a dream, which he wrote out and sent to the communities that remained.

For a book which depicts a great deal of violence, I find it striking how much peace is a theme. The central figure of the vision is a lamb, which looks as if it has been slain. All of the living world bows down to this lamb which has a sword for a tongue – it fights with its words. And after all the strong beasts of the world have tried and failed to open a sealed-up scroll, it is the lamb who succeeds in doing so. The scroll tells a story of horses and riders bent on conquest, who take peace from earth and make people kill one another. Poor wages and high prices follow, which leads to death and disease. Then there is an earthquake and everything goes dark. Everyone hides in the mountains and caves, preparing for what is to come.

I can't help but wonder if this represents John's experience. I also can't help but wonder at the extraordinary resonances in this letter with the climate crisis. In this 2000-year-old text John sees a future in which there are earthquakes, wildfires and sea level rises. He sees a third of the creatures that live in the sea going extinct, the water becoming polluted and people becoming sick from drinking it. He even sees that the key would be found for how to drill into the depths of the earth. From these depths he sees fumes being emitted which block out the sun and lead to a third of humanity being affected. But the part of humanity which is not affected doesn't turn away from what had caused the damage.

Then there is the system responsible for all this which John describes as *Babylon*, through which kings and merchants have become corrupted and unjustly wealthy. The spirit of Babylon is a dragon wearing seven crowns. It draws out of the sea an ugly beast who is put in charge of the empire. The beast builds great monuments and puts on great games. His image is placed on coins and people are made to worship it. Quaker writer Douglas Gwyn has compared the system this depicts to today's military industrial complex. The Archbishop of Canterbury, Justin Welby, calls it the "capital of capitalism".

But Babylon isn't the only force in the world. John sees a great movement building against it, chanting in unison. Then he sees the lamb again, this time on the Temple Mount, surrounded by thousands of people. The lamb and the dragon engage in a celestial battle which the lamb wins. A voice cries out that Babylon has fallen. Then seven figures dressed in white, carry bowls full of anguish for those who had abandoned God and worshipped the emperor and profited as merchants from the empire. Then he hears great crowds cheering and celebrating their freedom. In the crowd are all the people who had been killed because of their service to the movement.

And then there emerges a new heaven and a new earth, and a new Jerusalem, dressed like a bride at a wedding, irrigated by a river which quenches the Tree of Life. And a voice cries "there will be no more death or sorrow or crying or pain. All these things are gone forever."

For the old order of things has passed away.

Then I imagine John awaking from his dream and hurriedly scribing it and sending it out, his heart beating hard, a voice of hope for people resisting empire.

Then I imagine him remembering Jesus at his trial saying "my Kingdom is not of this world". Some – then and now – understood this to mean it exists only on a celestial plane. But in the light of the Bible as a whole, that isn't how I read it. I hear it more like a cry heard all over the world today among movements who are calling for justice:

"Another world is possible, another world is necessary, another world is coming."

# Epilogue

I suppose you could call what I've written in this book a political reading of the Bible. Given my education and background is in social movements, that assessment of my efforts would be fair. It isn't, however, my motivation. To read the Bible through the lens of the struggle is an interesting exercise, but the point is to then act on it. How could we see things the other way around, and read social change theologically today? How does the Bible read us?

In truth even avowedly secular progressive movements are often deeply – if subconsciously – religious. We speak of reformers spending long periods of time "in the wilderness", and when they challenge power being "crucified" by the press. The words "zeal" and "zealot" are used both positively and derogatorily depending who is using them. The metaphor of building "a new Jerusalem" to describe a world of justice and equality has sustained change-makers across generations. Many an activist has spoken – or sung – about "turning the world upside down" unaware of the origins of the phrase.

But the links are still stronger than that. I agree with the philosopher John MacMurray when he says that so-called "western civilisation" still essentially reflects the thought-structure of the Roman Empire. Although it often wears the clothes of Christianity with its roots in Hebrew thought and adorns itself with art borrowed from the Greeks, these represent little more than cultural appropriation, accepted only so far as they serve imperialism.

Karl Marx famously called this imperial religion the "opium of the people". Yet when people have been able to read the Bible for themselves, it has often presaged uprisings. England's Peasants' Revolt was encouraged by an egalitarian Christianity inspired by early translations of the Bible. In the same year as the Bible was published in German, an Anabaptist collective attempted to start a revolution to achieve a more communal system. In the centuries that followed, the Diggers, the Levellers, Chartists and abolitionists all took direct inspiration from the Bible as did many suffragist, socialist and anti-colonial movement leaders.

This helps explain why so many of the Bible's early translators into modern languages were persecuted. This oppression was not based on academic differences. It was about power. By putting this information in the hands of ordinary people, the translators were providing tools of liberation. When people read it, they found understandings which were very different from what the power-elites had said it was about.

In the Bible – as today – we find a struggle between two liturgies. In New Testament times the authorities made people worship Roman Emperors and their symbols. Today if someone prominent doesn't sing "God Save the Queen" or in the USA "God Bless America" they can expect to be widely criticised for it. In those times symbols representing Roman power were built all around the empire, which on occasion subjugated people rose up against. Today, even as I write these words, a global tug-of-war is raging between those who want their cities decorated with statues of racists, and others who want them pulled down.

These liturgies grow into contrasting beliefs. Many governments of the present, like Roman rulers of old, understand rights as applying principally – or only – to citizens. Against them stands a movement for universal human rights, recognising all people as children of God, including people from "over the river".

By writing these words I don't mean to fan the flames of polarisation. Rather I mean to point out that this difference in worldviews exists as a small part of working to resolve it. Rather than fuelling conflict and division, the Bible has the potential to act as a common vocabulary book, allowing people with different viewpoints to converse and try to understand one another better.

By one estimate there are up to five billion copies of the Bible in the world. That's five billion toolboxes for peace and liberation that exist across the planet, many of which remain unopened. This book is an invitation to pick one of them up. The fact that a great many of us don't is no doubt a relief to those who rule today's empires. Because if enough people studied and acted on Jesus' words, then the foundations of unjust power would start looking very sandy indeed.

# Notes and further reading

Even when working alone, the process of writing about ideas is collective, as we "converse" through the written word with others who shape our perspectives. These notes acknowledge some of those texts with pointers for further reading. In addition, I am grateful to Gerry Millar, Bridget Walker, Esther Leighton, Chloe Scaling, Beth Allen and others for feedback on early drafts and my family for conversations about it. All errors, of course, are my own. Bible quotes are from the New International Version unless indicated otherwise.

## Introduction

The question about whether Jesus is a teacher or a reformer is addressed in John MacMurray's *Search for Reality in Religion* (Friends Home Service, 1965). Walter Wink is one of the many who has eloquently emphasised Jesus' teaching on nonviolence (e.g., *The Powers That Be*, Galilee, 1998).

The Helen Steven quote is from her Swarthmore Lecture *No Extraordinary Power? Prayer, Stillness and Activism* (Quaker Books, 2005). The James Cone quote is from *A Black Theology of Liberation* (Orbis, 1970). The Desmond Tutu quote is used widely and seems to have originated from his evidence to the Eloff commission in 1982.

In *The Age of Reason* (1794) human rights pioneer Thomas Paine affirms his belief in God, the teachings of Jesus and the reality of divine revelation but says we can't reasonably call every word in the Bible the literal word of God because of the important contradictions between books. For saying this he was forced to flee the country.

The references to Rabbi Hillel and Augustine of Hippo are both from Karen Armstrong's *The Bible: The Biography* (Atlantic, 2015). Richard Rohr's method is set out in *What Do We Do with the Bible?* (SPCK, 2019). The Anthony Reddie quote is from *Is God Colour Blind? Insights from Black Theology for Christian Faith and Ministry* (SPCK, 2020 edition). The quote from Thomas Merton is used to introduce *The Pocket Thomas Merton* (Shambhala Press, 2017).

A seventeenth-century pamphlet for Quaker newcomers *Primitive Christianity Revived* (translated into modern English by Paul Buckley, Inner Light Books, 2018) reveals that Quakers have always used many words for God, including those cited, all of which have precedents in the Bible: the spirit (1 Corinthians 12:7), the word (Romans 10: 6–8), the truth within (John 14:6), the grace (Titus 2:11–12), the wisdom (Proverbs 1:20–23), the seed (1 Peter 1:23, 1 John 3:9), the revelation (Romans 1:19).

Love, joy, peace, patience, kindness, goodness, trustfulness, gentleness and self-control are the fruits of the spirit named by Paul in Galatians 5: 22–23.

## Chapter 1 – Lines of Dissent
## In the beginning

The Bible passages this section centres on are Genesis 1–4 and John 1 alongside 1 John: 4 7–21 ("God is love"). I'm grateful to Gill Sewell's enthusiasm for the radical implications of us all being made of stardust and to Mark Russ for drawing out the idea of Genesis as poetry. In 1920, the first World Conference of Friends affirmed the peace testimony as follows: "Can anyone who is truly sensitive to the Spirit of God working in him kill another man in whom he is convinced that the spirit is also working? If the answer is no, he will not therefore do nothing, he has found the ground common to both parties, and that ground the upon which an understanding and friendship may be built, namely the common Light and inspiration of God. Thus the belief in the Inward Light not only forbids war but opens up the true way of peace." (From *Quaker Writings*, Penguin, 2010).

In *A Dream of John Ball* (1888, Kelmscott) William Morris explores how the class equality in the Garden of Eden inspired later revolutionaries. Digger leader Gerrard Winstanley spoke of earth being created as "a common treasury to preserve beasts, birds, fishes and man" adding "but not one word was spoken in the beginning that one branch of mankind should rule over another". Sarah and Angelina Grimkè were inspired by the gender equality before the fall and abolitionist John Woolman spoke of it as a time before people developed self-serving intentions "to get the upperhand of their fellow creatures".

Pope Francis' Encyclical Letter *Laudato si '* (Vatican documents, 2015) includes a chapter on ecology and the creation before discussing Jesus' environmental outlook. Eden Grace locates a Quaker eco-theology in George Fox's writings on life before the fall (See *On Earth as it is in Heaven,* Swarthmore Lecture, 2019) as does Stuart Masters in the works of James Nayler (Friends Quarterly, Issue 1, 2020). Pam Lunn's 2011 Swarthmore Lecture *Costing Not Less Than Everything* can be watched online and the book version is available from Quaker Books.

## Noah's Ark

The story of Noah's Ark is told in Genesis 5–9.

The book by Symon Hill mentioned is the *No-Nonsense Guide to Religion* (New Internationalist, 2010). Novelist Hilary Mantel pithily makes the same point in her 2017 Reith Lecture when she says "Mythology is not fiction but truth dressed up in symbol".

The science fiction books mentioned are *War of the Worlds* by HG Wells (William Heineman, 1897), *Day of the Triffids* by John Wyndham (Michael Joseph, 1951) and *Parable of the Talents* by Octavia Butler (Seven Stories Press, 1998).

I enjoyed the podcast *Two Feminists Annotate the Bible* for critical engagement with the more patriarchal aspects of Noah's story. I'm grateful to Mart Layton for thoughts on what it says about animals. I'm also an admirer of the Operation

Noah campaign for Christian action on climate change whose approach may well have influenced this reflection.

## Abram and Sarai

This story is told through Genesis 10–50 then reiterated in Acts 7, Romans 4 and Hebrews 11.

For a description of the Standard of Ur see *A History of the World in 100 Objects* (Allen Lane, 2010).

## Freedom from Slavery

This reflection is based on the books of Exodus, Leviticus, Numbers, Deuteronomy and Joshua.

Other works mentioned are Nelson Mandela's *Long Walk to Freedom* (Abacus, 1994), Martin Luther King Jr's *Autobiography* (Ed. Clayborne Carson, Abacus, 2000), Albert Luthuli's *Let My People Go* (Fontana, 1962) and Ralph Abernathy's *And the Walls Came Tumbling Down* (Chicago Review Press, 2010). The 2019 biopic *Harriet* (dir. Kasi Lemmons) tells Harriet Tubman's story. Mahalia Jackson's rendition of *Joshua Fit the Battle of Jericho* is available online. It's notable that this theme is echoed in the title of Barack Obama's Presidential memoir *A Promised Land* (2020).

## Power

This section reflects on Joshua 6–24, Judges, 1 Samuel, 2 Samuel, 1 Kings, 2 Kings, 1 Chronicles, 2 Chronicles, Psalms, Proverbs, Ecclesiastes and Song of Songs. For an account of how the Bible was written see Karen Armstrong *The Bible: The Biography*, Atlantic, 2015.

Particularly troubling sections of these include the stories of Tamar the princess (2 Samuel 13:1–22), the unnamed concubine (Judges 19: 1–30) and the daughter of Jephthah (Judges 11:29–40). Feminist scholar Phyllis Trible argues that the Bible deliberately "recounts tales of terror in memoriam to offer sympathetic readings of abused women ... and to pray that those terrors shall not come to pass again" (cited in Susan Durber, *Preaching Like a Woman*, SPCK, 2007).

For an honest but unflattering account of Quakers' mixed record on racial justice see Donna McDaniel and Vanessa Julye's *Fit for Freedom Not for Friendship* (FGC, 2010).

## Prophets

This section reflects on the books of Ruth, Ezra, Nehemiah, Esther, Isaiah, Jeremiah, Ezekiel, Hosea, Joel, Amos, Micah, Zephaniah, Habakkuk and Malachi. The specific quotes are from Amos 5: 21–23, Hosea 12:7, Micah 6:8, Isaiah 2:4, Habakkuk 2:11 (NLT), Malachi 2:3 (NLT) and Psalm 146 (KJV). Martin Luther King Jr quoted Amos 5:24. The speech also references Isaiah 40: 4-5.

The apostles were also accused – pejoratively – of trying to turn the world upside down (see Acts 17:1–6), as were early Quakers among others (see Christopher Hill, *The World Turned Upside Down*, Penguin, 1972). The phrase is also the title of a song by Leon Rosselson.

## Radical Jesus

### Origins

This section centres on Matthew 1–3 and Luke 2 (Jesus' birth) informed by Luke 1:52–53 (Mary's song), Isaiah 2:4 (swords into ploughshares), Isaiah 9:6 (Prince of Peace) and Mark 13:55 (Jesus' siblings). Judas the Galilean is mentioned in Acts 5:37 and the revolt of Judas the Maccabean is told in 1 Maccabees (Catholic and Orthodox Bibles). Joshua's story is told in the books of Moses and of course in the Book of Joshua.

The insight about Jesus' likely original name comes from Diarmaid MacCulloch's *A History of Christianity: the first 3000 years* (Penguin, 2010), and the historical commentary comes from Reza Aslan's *Zealot: The Life and Times of Jesus of Nazareth*

(Random House, 2013) cross-referenced with *Antiquities of the Jews* by Josephus. Robert Beckford's 2006 TV series *The Secret Family of Jesus* offers thoughts as to why the church over the years has played down the role of Jesus' family.

## John the Baptist

John the Baptist's story is told in all four Gospels, notably Mark 1 and 6, Matthew 3 and 14, Luke 1, 3, 7 and 9 and John 1. John's instruction to soldiers to do violence to no one is from Luke 3:14 (KJV). Historical context is drawn from Reza Aslan's biography of Jesus. At least one zealot, Simon, became a disciple of Jesus.

## Wilderness

The story of Jesus in the wilderness is told in Matthew 4:1–11, Mark 1:12–13 and Luke 4:1–13. Context on wilderness and the "desert fathers" comes from Diarmaid MacCulloch's *A History of Christianity: The first 3000 years* (Penguin, 2010).

My Granny Joyce believed we are each wisest as babies before society and our egos combine to distort our intuitive connection with the cosmos, but that we retain a "wordless knowing" (Joyce Gee, "Wordless Knowing", *The Friend,* 25/10/18). 1 Kings 19:12 speaks of the "still small voice". The opening lines of the Quaker book of Advices and Queries talks about "the promptings of love and truth" in the heart, to be understood as the leadings of God.

James Baldwin (*Dark Days,* 1980/Penguin, 2018) and Thomas Merton (Shambhala, 2017) both talk about the masks imposed on us by others from birth. In *Poetry Is Not a Luxury* (1977, reprinted in *The Masters Tools Will Never Dismantle the Master's House,* Penguin 2018) Audre Lorde speaks of the counterhegemonic value of listening to the inward voice when it says "it feels right to me".

In *The Crossway* (Picador, 2018) Guy Stagg quotes a French nun, Sister Marie Bertille who calls pilgrimage and monastic life two expressions of the same impulse. He also cites Bernard of Clairvaux who believed that monastic life was also a pilgrimage, as "even though he stayed in one place, he travelled with his heart".

It's notable that John Bunyan's *The Pilgrim's Progress* was written while in prison. The early Quakers of the same period also spent a great deal of time in prison, interspersed by long journeys on foot. It was while incarcerated that George Fox wrote the letter in which he spoke about "walking cheerfully over the world" (Quaker Faith and Practice, 19:32). "I am available to what seeks to emerge in, through and as me" is part of a meditation by Michael Bernard Beckwith.

## The beginnings of the movement

This section centres on the Sermon on the Mount, expressed in Matthew 5–7 (also referred to as the Sermon on the Plain at Luke 6:17–49).

There are those who have read these words and suggested that Jesus couldn't have possibly meant what he said, because doing so would be impractical or even "impossible". Others have suggested that these are teachings only for some – perhaps the clergy or monks – or apply to a future life rather than this one. I don't think these approaches hold water. The Sermon on the Mount is addressed to the multitudes – the masses – and contains guidance still relevant to movements today. Why on earth would Jesus teach impossible ideas?

It's true that when living under systems imbued with injustice, conforming to how things are can lead to complicity with violence. As a result, inadvertently doing harm can be more straightforward than doing good. But Jesus asks us to "repent" which means to turn around and go in a different direction. In that sense, then, doing good is an act of rebellion.

These were the parts of the Bible that first compelled my attention, deepened through reading my grandad's copies of

Leo Tolstoy's *What I Believe* and *The Kingdom of God Is Within You* (OUP, 1885 and 1894). I'm also inspired by the Catholic Worker movement, whose co-founder Dorothy Day (see *The Long Loneliness*, Harper Collins, 1952) once declared "Our manifesto is the Sermon on the Mount" and Keir Hardie who described it as more radical than any political platform (*From Serfdom to Socialism*, 1907, repr. L & W 2015). The blogs and podcasts of the Red-Letter Christians in the US have also been helpful.

Susan Durber's advice is reflected in the introduction to *Of the Same Flesh: Exploring a Theology of Gender* (Christian Aid, 2014). I'm also grateful to another former colleague, John Cooper, now Director of the UK Fellowship of Reconciliation, for introducing me to the work of Elias Chacour. Comments on the word "blessed" are from *We Belong to the Land* (University of Notre Dame Press, 2000). The Barrington Dunbar quote is from *A Reaction to the Believers Church Conference*, first published in 1970, reprinted in *Black Fire: African American Quakers on Spirituality and Human Rights* (FGC, 2011).

## A social view of disability

This section looks at the healing miracles which take place in all four Gospels. In preparing it, I found Naomi Lawson Jacobs' research summary *The Upside-Down Kingdom of Heaven* helpful (see naomilawsonjacobs.com).

The incident with Legion and the pigs is from Mark 5:1–20, and Luke 8:26–39. The interpretation given to this is strongly shaped by Ched Myers' *Binding the Strong Man* (Orbis, 2008). For more on colonial society affecting mental health, see the scholarship of Franz Fanon.

The idea that when Peter accompanies a disabled man in Acts 3:2 he is supporting him into a part of the Temple he had been excluded from has been discussed by many, of whom Gordon Temple is one, see *Enabling Church: towards the Full Inclusion of Disabled People* (SPCK, 2012).

Among others, Tom Shakespeare has highlighted Hebrews 12:13 "make level paths for your feet, so that the lame may not be disabled, but rather, healed" as applicable to wheelchair ramps, see *Openings to the Infinite Ocean* (Quaker Books, 2020). The risen Christ as wounded is explored in Nancy L Eisland's *The Disabled God: Toward a Liberatory Theology of Disability* (Abingdon, 1994). The quote from Becky Tyler comes from a 2019 BBC article titled "Stop Trying to Heal Me", and refers to Daniel 7:9 and Ezekiel 1:15–26. Paralympic Athlete Jean Driscoll has also talked about God's wheelchair.

The conference mentioned was *Telling Encounters: Stories of Disability, Faith and God*, September 2020, organised by Inclusive Church and St Martin-in-the-Fields.

## Gender Equality

We meet Mary Magdalene in Luke 8:2–3. References to her presence at the cross, the tomb, and encountering the risen Christ can be found at Matthew 27:55–56, 27:61 and 28:1, Mark 15:40–41, 15:40–47 and 16:1, Luke 24:10 and John 20. From the sixth to the twentieth centuries the Catholic Church taught that she was a prostitute, but this has since been rescinded. The recent feature film *Mary Magdalene* (dir. Garth Davis) presents a refreshingly different account centring her leadership role.

The teachings about women and the Kingdom of Heaven/ Kingdom of God are at Matthew 25:1–13, Luke 15:8–10 and Matthew 13:33. The widow's offering at the Temple is at Mark 12:41–44 and Luke 21:1–4. The story of the woman of Samaria is told at John 4:4–24. The story of the woman rumoured to be a sex worker is told at Luke 36–50 (I say rumoured because it implies but never quite says that she is). The story about the women accused of adultery is found at John 8:1–11.

This section draws strongly on Margaret Fell's *Women's Ministry Justified* (1666, reprinted in *Quaker Writings: An Anthology*, Penguin 2010). Fell further cites Genesis 3, Acts 2:16–

18 and Revelation 12 in support of her case, as well as pointing out the various women who served with Paul. *The Quaker Bible Reader* (ESR, 2006) develops this case. Susan Durber's *Preaching Like a Woman* (SPCK, 2007) explores women's ministry as feminist theology. Womanist theologian Jacqueline Grant's *White Women's Christ and Black Women's Jesus* (AAR, 1989) looks at the intersections with race and class. Esther Mombo's quote is in both the *Quaker Bible Reader* and her chapter in *Scriptures in Dialogue: Christians and Muslims Reading the Bible and the Koran Together* (Church House Publishing 2003). Marcella Althaus-Reid's quote is in *From Feminist Theology to Indecent Theology*, SCM Press, 2004, quoted in *Preaching Like a Woman*.

The extra-biblical texts mentioned can be found in *The Gnostic Gospels* (Sacred Texts, 2005). These have been a source of inspiration for Christian feminists including the Quaker Women's Group who co-wrote *Bringing the Invisible into the Light* (Swarthmore Lecture, 1986) and Elaine Pagels whose best-known book on the Gnostic texts was published in 1979.

Whilst writing this chapter, I held in mind the message of *Letters to a Broken Church* (Ekklesia, 2019) which shines a light on clerical abuse and failures of safeguarding, and calls for a spiritually rooted change.

## Racial justice

The parable of the Good Samaritan can be found in Luke 10:25–37. The story of the Samaritan woman is at John 4:4–26. We meet the first faithful Roman centurion in Matthew 8:5–13. We meet the second faithful Roman soldier, Cornelius, in Acts 10. The origins of the people who were among the earliest Christians can be found at Acts 2: 9–10.

When talking these ideas through with my partner, she suggested that the debate about Cornelius joining the movement might be similar to a serving white police officer joining a Black Lives Matter group.

Symon Hill's *The Upside Down Bible* (DLT, 2005) explores the Good Samaritan as an anti-racist story, and also suggests it could be called "The Good Muslim". James Cone quotes are from *The Cross and the Lynching Tree* (Orbis, 2013).

## Class

Bible verses referred to in this reflection include Matthew 6:9 (Lord's prayer), Matthew 23 ("Woe to you teachers of the law and Pharisees"), Mark 6:3 (Jesus the carpenter), Acts 4:13 (Peter and John as "unschooled, ordinary men"), Luke 1:48 (Mary the servant girl, NLT), Matthew 25:14–30 (Parable of the Talents), Luke 6:24 ("Woe to you who are rich"), Luke 11: 37–54 (Woes on the pharisees and experts), Matthew 24:36 (the day or hour), Luke 17: 20–21 NLT ("The Kingdom of God is already among you") and 1 John 3:18 (love with action) and the letter of James.

The jubilee of debt cancellation is explained in Leviticus 25, which forms the biblical inspiration for the Jubilee Debt Campaign. The Parable of the Talents from the perspective of the servant is explored in *Surprised by Grace* by Susan Durber (Granary, 2013) who explains that sometimes in rich countries preachers have suggested that the master in the story represents God and the servant is to blame for his poverty. In contrast, in parts of the Middle East it is said that congregations cheer for the servant's resistance. The questions about the Ebionites are from *James, Brother of Jesus* by Alan Saxby (Wipf and Stock, 2015). A Leveller statement in the seventeenth century declared that "The relation of master and servant has no ground in the New Testament ... There is no ground in nature or scripture why one man should have £1000 per annum, another not £1." This was echoed by John Woolman, in *A Caution to the Rich* (1793, usually printed as an appendix to his Journal), who proposed respect for indigenous peoples, rent controls, shorter work days, wealth redistribution, migrants rights and work for peace as a means of enabling James' vision.

Twentieth-century works exploring the Bible and economic justice include *Theology for the Social Gospel* by Walter Rauschenbusch (Leopold Classics, 1917), *A Theology of Liberation* by Gustavo Gutierrez (SCM, 1971) and *Jesus Christ Liberator* by Leonardo Boff (Orbis, 1978). Both Gutierrez and Boff faced opposition from church hierarchies for their writings, on the basis that they sound similar to socialism. Pope Francis, however, has praised the spirit of Liberation Theology, and reflected some of its themes in his encyclicals.

Towards the end of his life Friedrich Engels offered a respectful exegesis of Christian thought and its working-class and revolutionary foundations, see *On the Origins of Early Christianity* (1894). Rather more disingenuously Leon Trotsky paraphrased a number of Jesus' sayings in his speeches, ("We stand as a city on the mount", "men of little faith", "we shall create such a paradise ... upon earth") even while mobilising for war (*A Word to the Russian Workers and Peasants on Our Friends and Enemies*, 1918).

In *Strength to Love* (1963) Martin Luther King Jr offered a level-headed engagement with Marxist thought, affirming that any form of state Communism so far seen is inconsistent with Christianity, but praising the commitment to the disenfranchised that inspires left-wing activists. After a similarly serious investigation, John MacMurray wondered whether modern socialist movements might represent that part of Christianity abandoned by Constantine but now reasserting itself once again (*Search for Reality in Religion*, 1965).

## LGBTQIA+ Equality

Bible passages referred to in this section are Matthew 8:5 and Luke 7:1–10 (faith of the Roman centurion), Matthew 19:12 (instruction not to be prejudiced against eunuchs) and Matthew 17:1–8, Mark 9:2–8, Luke 9:28–36 (the transfiguration). Also, Genesis 2:7 (nonbinary Adam), Genesis 37:3 (Joseph's coat of many colours), 1 Samuel 18:1–4 (Jonathan and David), the Book of Ruth (Ruth and Naomi) and the Song of Songs. The deeper reading of "Love your neighbour as yourself" comes from *Towards a Quaker View of Sex* (Friends Home Service, 1963) which was one of the earliest publications by a church to promote a positive view of homosexuality. In present times, Peterson Toscano's presentations have been particularly helpful in helping me engage with eunuchs in the Bible, see Petersontoscano.com.

Patrick Cheng's introduction to queer theology *Radical Love* (Church Publishing, 2011) gives an overview of scholarship in this area.

## Protest

This section covers the events told in Matthew 21–26, Mark 11–14, Luke 19:28–22:52 and John 12:12–18:12. Each writer has the events in a slightly different order, so I've broadly followed the narrative of Matthew. Thoughts on the protection of the crowd were influenced by John Dominic Crossan in his piece "Why did Jesus go to Jerusalem?", 31/3/12, *Huffington Post*.

## Prisoner of conscience

This section centres on Matthew 26:57–27:56, Mark 14:53–15:40, Luke 22:54–23:49 and John 18:1–19:38.

A helpful exploration of Amnesty's origin story is offered by Bill Shipsey in "The toast to freedom that led to Amnesty International", *Huffington Post*, 6/12/17.

The term "Prisoner of Conscience" is attributed to Eric Baker. The statement from his own tribunal as a conscientious objector is in *Quaker Faith and Practice* 24:14. In an 1897 Christmas message, Keir Hardie described seeing the image of Christ in every hungry child. In *The Cross and the Lynching Tree* (Orbis, 2013) James Cone draws connections between lynching and the crucifixion.

## The Activism of the Apostles

This section centres on Matthew 28, Mark 16, Luke 24, John 20 and Acts 2:1–12.

"Don't Mourn, Organise" is based on the words of trade union leader Joe Hill (1875–1915), and is expressed in the "Ballad of Joe Hill", sung by Paul Robeson among many others. "You can kill the revolutionary but not the revolution" is a quote from former Black Panther Deputy Chairman Fred Hampton who was assassinated by Chicago police in 1969. "She is a seed that has multiplied" is a slogan used after the assassination of Berta Càceres in 2016. Originating in Mozambique's liberation struggle, the Portuguese language slogan "A Luta Continua" (the struggle continues) has been used by many movements. It is now common to hear it in Spanish as "La Lucha Continua".

The slogan "to each according to his need from each according to his ability to pay" has a biblical forebear in Acts 2:44–45.

## Peter

Jesus calls Peter a rock at Matthew 16:18 and a stumbling block at 16:23. The story of Peter's denial is told in Matthew 26:33–35, Mark 14:29–31 and 69–70, Luke 22:33–34 and 22:54–57, and John 13:36–38 and 18:13–27. Jesus tells Peter to put down his sword in Matthew 16:18 and John 18:11. What the apostles did next is narrated in Acts 1–6. "Think it possible you are mistaken" forms part of Advices and Queries 17 in *Quaker Faith and Practice* 1:02.

Put Down the Sword is a faith-based direct-action group which has protested at arms fairs and weapons factories in the UK.

## Paul

Paul's story is told in Acts:8–28 and the letters 1 Thessalonians, Galatians, 1 Corinthians, 2 Corinthians, Philemon, Philippians and Romans. Direct quotes are from 1 Corinthians 13:12, 2 Corinthians 11:17 and Romans 7:14–24.

The idea to read Paul's letters in order comes from Marcus Borg. The biographer of Paul mentioned is Tom Wright, whose book *Paul: A Biography* (SPCK, 2018) is quoted. Steve Chalke (*The Lost Message of Paul*, SPCK, 2019) also offers an interesting exploration of Paul's ideas as does Timothy Peat-Ashworth in *Heaven on Earth* (Plain Press, 2018).

## Resilience

Direct Bible quotes in order are from 2 Corinthians 1:8, 2 Corinthians 4:1–12, James 1:2–4, Philippians 2:14–15, Philippians 1:9, Philippians 4:8, Philippians 2:3, Philippians 4:2, James 4:14, Luke 17:21 (NLT), Philippians 3:20–21 and 1 Peter 2:9 (KJV). The two modern books mentioned are *Hope in the Dark* by Rebecca Solnit (Canongate, 2016) and *The Age of Overwhelm* by Laura van Dernoot Lipsky (Berret-Koehler, 2018).

Earlier generations of Quakers put particular emphasis on being God's people/"a peculiar people" see Douglas Gwyn *Peace Finds the Purpose of a Peculiar People* (Inner Light Books, 2016).

## The Book of Revolution

Revelation was particularly important to early Quakers, including George Fox, Margaret Fell and James Nayler. In interpreting it, I found Douglas Gwyn's *Militant Peacemaking in the Manner of Friends* (Inner Light, 2016) helpful as well as *Resisting Empire* by C Wess Daniels (Barclay Press, 2020) whose work also influenced the Epilogue. The quote from Justin Welby is from *Dethroning Mammon* (Bloomsbury, 2017).

## Epilogue

Well-known historical reformers who connected their activism to their understanding of the Bible include Digger Gerrard Winstanley, Leveller John Lilburne, Chartist Ernest Jones, women's equality advocates Margaret Fell, Mary Wollstonecraft and Anne Knight and abolitionists including Olaudah Equiano,

Sojourner Truth and Lucretia Mott. Among activists eventually elected as politicians are Britain's first socialist MP Keir Hardie, first female mayor in London Ada Salter and longest serving MP Tony Benn, all of whom wrote about their admiration for the Bible as did African freedom struggle leaders Kwame Nkrumah, Julius Nyerere and Kenneth Kaunda who became Presidents of Ghana, Tanzania and Zambia after independence.

The John MacMurray quote is from *Freedom in the Modern World* (Faber, 1932).

## THE NEW OPEN SPACES

Throughout the two thousand years of Christian tradition there
have been, and still are, groups and individuals that exist in
the margins and upon the edge of faith. But in Christianity's
contrapuntal history it has often been these outcasts and
pioneers that have forged contemporary orthodoxy out
of former radicalism as belief evolves to engage with and
encompass the ever-changing social and scientific realities. Real
faith lies not in the comfortable certainties of the Orthodox,
but somewhere in a half-glimpsed hinterland on the dirt track
to Emmaus, where the Death of God meets the Resurrection,
where the supernatural Christ meets the historical Jesus,
and where the revolution liberates both the oppressed and
the oppressors.

Welcome to Christian Alternative... a space at the edge where
the light shines through.
If you have enjoyed this book, why not tell other readers by
posting a review on your preferred book site.

## Christian Atheist
Belonging without Believing
Brian Mountford
Christian Atheists don't believe in God but miss him: especially
the transcendent beauty of his music, language, ethics, and
community.
Paperback: 978-1-84694-439-0 ebook: 978-1-84694-929-6

## Compassion Or Apocalypse?
A Comprehensible Guide to the Thoughts of René Girard
James Warren
How René Girard changes the way we think about God and the
Bible, and its relevance for our apocalypse-threatened world.
Paperback: 978-1-78279-073-0 ebook: 978-1-78279-072-3

## Diary Of A Gay Priest
The Tightrope Walker
Rev. Dr. Malcolm Johnson
Full of anecdotes and amusing stories, but the Church is still a
dangerous place for a gay priest.
Paperback: 978-1-78279-002-0 ebook: 978-1-78099-999-9

## Do You Need God?
Exploring Different Paths to Spirituality Even For Atheists
Rory J.Q. Barnes
An unbiased guide to the building blocks of spiritual belief.
Paperback: 978-1-78279-380-9 ebook: 978-1-78279-379-3

Readers of ebooks can buy or view any of these bestsellers by clicking on the live link in the title. Most titles are published in paperback and as an ebook. Paperbacks are available in traditional bookshops. Both print and ebook formats are available online.

Find more titles and sign up to our readers' newsletter at
http://www.johnhuntpublishing.com/christianity
Follow us on Facebook at
https://www.facebook.com/ChristianAlternative